To Sea Oar
Knot To Sea

A novice at sailing
An ocean awaiting

Andrew Diggins

Bright Pen

A Bright Pen Book

British Library Cataloguing Publication Data.
A catalogue record for this book is available from the British
Library

ISBN 978-0-7552-1639-0

Authors OnLine Ltd
19 The Cinques
Gamlingay, Sandy
Bedfordshire SG19 3NU
England

This book is also available in e-book format, details of which
are available at www.authorsonline.co.uk

Contents

Acknowledgement

My grateful thanks
to my brother Chris
for offering me the opportunity to sail an ocean,
to my new sailing buddies Robin and Glyn
for encouraging me to take it,
to the World Cruising Club
for making the whole thing possible,
and to my dear wife Maureen
for being simply the best friend
a man could have.

Preface

If you are a serious sailor looking to me to teach you more,
then this book is not for you.
If you want clarity about schooners and sloops, cutters and
ketches,
then this book is not for you.
If it annoys you when people still give measurements in feet
and inches,
then this book is not for you.
But if you want a glimpse of what it is like to sail a vast ocean
on a small yacht,
then this book could well be for you.
It is a simple tale of four over-fifties coming together to sail a
forty-two foot yacht across the Atlantic Ocean as part of the
2013 Atlantic Rally for Cruisers.
It is a snapshot of a year in our lives,
from signing up through to crossing the finishing line.
It tells of our aspirations, preparations, observations,
consternations and celebrations.
It is written from my perspective, the novice of the four.
If by chance, you too are a novice but have the opportunity
to sail,
I hope this book encourages you.
And if by chance this book discourages you from sailing,
then bin it and do it anyway!

Andrew

To Sea Oar Knot To Sea

A novice at sailing
An ocean awaiting

Chapter One

The yacht, the crew, and a novice's view

The shrouded invitation

"Behind every one of these windows is somebody who might be a horse-jumping champion, a formula one racing champion, a yachtsman of high degree, but he'll never know because he'll never step on a yacht or formula one car – he'll never get the chance." (Billy Connolly recalling the words of shipworkers' union boss Jimmy Reid at his funeral tribute, August 2010.)

Given the opportunity to sail the Atlantic Ocean on a 40 foot yacht, thousands of people would jump at the chance. But Jimmy Reid knew, looking up with comedian Billy Connolly at row upon row of featureless windows in a high-rise tenement block, that such an opportunity would never arise for the vast majority of people in that building and in countless other buildings like it. For a fortunate few, such a chance comes along perhaps just once in a lifetime. I am one of that fortunate few. And to my way of thinking, if I had turned down that chance, I would somehow have let down those unknown thousands who would have traded places with me in the blink of an eye, if only their circumstances were different. So I said 'Yes'.

For me, the 'once in a lifetime' day was the 10th November 2012. It happened like this. Four of us were enjoying a meal together at a local restaurant in our home town of Reigate in Surrey. Around the table were my brother, Chris, his wife, Angela, my wife, Maureen and me. We were celebrating my brother's birthday. And for Chris, this particular birthday was a biggie; he had turned 60. As we ate, I took every opportunity to pepper the conversation with quips and anecdotes about senior citizenship and senility. I knew that I could keep up such ridicule, on and off, for the next two-and-a-half years until I too reached that milestone age.

So it was over a dinner table that I had said 'Yes' to my brother's question that in its delivery was more like an ambush. Chris had deployed the same technique used on Wednesdays at Prime Minister's Questions in the House of Commons. The tradition is that Members of Parliament start by asking the Prime Minister an innocuous question about his diary for the day. Actually, they are not remotely interested in his plans, but it gives them the opportunity to ask a supplementary question, the real question that they want answered. However, we all know that wanting an answer and getting an answer are two completely different things in our Houses of Parliament. Politicians in general and Prime Ministers in particular seem to be born with an innate inability to give a straight answer to a straight question. But I am no politician, so when Chris set the trap, I was snared.

The innocuous question was my brother asking when our visits abroad were going to be over the next year; he knew that Maureen and I were routinely away from home. When we retired early in 2010, among other things, we volunteered to lead tours of Israel and Palestine three times each year. I duly answered my brother that we would be in the Middle East during February, August and September and so opened myself up to that all important supplementary question. "Good," he said, "so you are free to sail the Atlantic with us in November next year, aren't you?" By 'us' he meant himself and two of his sailing buddies. He was right; I was free. And even though I was a novice at sailing, compared with Chris and his two friends, I readily agreed without any serious thought of what may lay ahead.

Bizarrely, as our conversation inevitably turned to the sailing adventure Chris had in mind, the very first question that came to me had nothing to do with sailing competence or personal safety but rather, whether I was likely to gain or lose weight as a result of being on a small boat for so long. I reasoned to myself that it could go either way. On the one hand, I knew that my posture would be constantly adjusting itself to compensate for the yacht's movement over three or more weeks at sea, and I was certain that such prolonged muscle-movement was likely to shed pounds from my frame. On the other hand, I guessed there would be lengthy periods of inactivity with nothing to do but nibble, having the opposite effect on my waistline. It was, of course, a question impossible to answer as we enjoyed that celebratory meal, but I knew I would find out in due course, and I promise to share the answer with you.

The Captain and his crew

Chris was the skipper. No-one could argue with that because he was also the owner of the yacht, a Moody 425 called Second Wind. Now semi-retired, Chris spent his career as an engineer focused on all things electronic connected with air traffic control. His gifted ability with electronics surfaced early in our childhood. When he was barely into his teenage years, he reconfigured an old valve wireless that stood in the corner of the family living room. His adaptation allowed us boys to monitor from our upstairs bedroom every word being said downstairs by our parents after we had gone up to bed, supposedly out of earshot. When he was found out, I remember dad being very impressed and mum being very cross! With that ability to secretly intercept private conversations, it is a wonder that Chris chose a career in air traffic control rather than with the News of the World.

Robin was second in command and in his early fifties. By day he is the proprietor of a long-established Surrey-based auction house dealing in art, antiques and collectables. On several occasions, his saleroom has been featured on the daytime television favourite, Bargain Hunt. By night, Robin indulges his passion and talent for music, being the vocalist and lead guitar player in a heavy rock band called Dark Ages. Those who go to his gigs love them. Those who live next door to his gigs are not so keen. Robin also loves fish, knows a bit about fishing and was determined to catch us some dinner when we crossed the ocean.

Glyn hates fish. Also in his early fifties, Glyn works mainly from home, project managing the installation of new telephony systems. He was perhaps the most diligent of all of us in preparing himself for the adventure, reading many books, visiting many websites and creating many spreadsheets. Glyn also happens to be type-one diabetic, which makes his diet more important than ours. Partly because of this, and partly because he wanted to, Glyn volunteered to look after the provisioning of Second Wind for the voyage, which broadly meant working out the quantities of food and drink required and overseeing the process of buying it all.

So, in addition to the question of whether I would gain or lose weight, two more questions arose: Would Robin catch a fish? Would Glyn eat it?

Chris and Robin had met when they both sailed dinghies

at a local club as a weekend leisure activity. Subsequently they both studied and passed their Yacht Master (Coastal) sailing qualifications. Glyn has qualified as a Coastal Skipper. All three have known each other for several years and have sailed together a number of times, either chartering a yacht for a weekend in the Solent or sometimes enjoying a holiday afloat in the Mediterranean. Compared with a voyage across the Atlantic, their sailing experiences had been gained over relatively short distances and calm waters.

Then there was me. My career had been in financial services, specialising in communications and culminating in becoming a ghost-writer for the company directors, drafting their articles, pronouncements, speeches, and so on. The downside to this was that they got the credit for all my good work. The upside was that they had to shoulder the blame for all my bad work! I held no formal qualifications in sailing (or in anything else for that matter) but I am drawn to boats and have enjoyed a handful of sailing holidays, mainly on the west coast of Scotland, which is simply beautiful. I may have taken turns at the helm or helped with the sails but only under the watchful eye of the skippers. I was never responsible for anything. Without doubt, I was the novice of the four.

Given our diverse backgrounds, careers, experiences and hobbies, it was not surprising that the four of us were quite different in so many respects. However, we shared a pleasure of being on boats and relished the prospect of achieving the Atlantic challenge together. So what could possibly galvanise such an unlikely quartet into a lean, mean sailing machine? The 2013 London Boat Show revealed the obvious answer to Robin. He bought us all matching T-Shirts with the yacht name embroidered on them. That would do it! That was the first essential expenditure. Many more essential expenditures would follow before we would set off on our adventure.

The Atlantic Rally for Cruisers

Sailing across the Atlantic Ocean is undoubtedly a challenge for anyone but we would not be doing it alone. Chris had entered us and his yacht into the 2013 Annual Rally for Cruisers (ARC). The first ARC rally was sailed in 1986 and was so successful that, as a result, the World Cruising Club was formed and the trans-Atlantic rally became an annual event. In recent times, it has attracted upward of 200 yachts each year, some long and luxurious, some quite modest in size and comfort, and many in between.

Participating yachts depart from the large marina complex in Las Palmas, Gran Canaria during the month of November and set a course for Rodney Bay in Saint Lucia. But as the ever-discerning Captain Jack Sparrow says in the Pirates of the Caribbean film, 'On Stranger Tides', "It's not the destination so much as the journey, they say." Lovely as Saint Lucia is as a destination, it is the journey to get there that is at the heart of the ARC, a journey of some 2,800 nautical miles. There is no prescribed route and skippers judge for themselves what compass bearing best suits their vessels, their aspirations, their nerves and the weather conditions. The majority of yachts follow the course of the prevailing trade winds, first heading south, keeping parallel with the west coast of Africa, before turning west towards the Caribbean.

Although the route to take may be up for debate, the Club's experience and expertise are beyond question. Since its inception, it has overseen more than 5,000 craft across the ocean. They know the best time of the year to make the crossing and give sensible guidance to ensure that boats and their crews are as prepared as they should be for the challenge. But they also know how to make the whole event fun for everyone, with onshore activities both before the start and after arrival.

The greatest feature of the rally is that it opens up ocean sailing to people who would otherwise never pluck up the courage for such a voyage, or would not have a notion of how to plan and prepare for it themselves. People like me, in fact. The rally routinely attracts people of all ages and differing levels of experience; young and old, male and female, families and friends, experienced and novices, all are welcomed.

Rally or race?

So is it a rally or is it a race? Quite simply, it depends on who you ask. The crew of the yacht that crosses the finishing line first will be earnest that not only is it a race, but it is one of the most important races of the annual sailing calendar. However, the crew of the boat that arrives in Saint Lucia after everyone else has gone home for Christmas will be equally earnest that it is just a bit of fun and, anyway, they deliberately went slow so they could enjoy the sea-scenery for longer.

In fact, there is not just one winner, as the organisers divide the ARC rally yachts into three divisions. The vast majority of crews enter themselves into the Cruising Division. The only thing that boats in this category are compelled to have in common is just one hull; monohulls, as they are called.

Vessels with more than one hull such as catamarans sail in the Multihull Division. The boats in both of these divisions are not normally built for racing but are nevertheless sufficiently robust for the rigours of ocean sailing.

The third category is the Racing Division. Those in this division start on the same day and aim for the same finishing line as everyone else, but they sail under slightly different rules and the boats tend to be built for speed rather than comfort. For example, crews are unlikely to sleep on comfortable mattresses; their beds may be nothing more than a piece of fabric slung between two poles. Flushing toilets are another weighty luxury that they may have to do without, crews adopting instead what is known as the 'bucket and chuck it' method of sanitation. Drinking water is also very heavy and so only the minimum required would be carried, crews relying on watermakers to desalinate sea water for anything extra. Similarly, they may well have to live on dehydrated ration packs rather than carrying any bulky fresh produce.

The only extra weight that is willingly carried is in their sails compartment. It is common for racing yachts to carry an array of sails suitable for every strength of wind that they may encounter, enabling them to keep moving in any conditions except for no wind at all. A flat calm with no breath of breeze is a racing crew's nightmare. It matters not that their yacht may have cost a King's ransom; if there is no wind, it is not going anywhere.

Ask the 'race or rally' question to any of those in racing crews and they will be in no doubt that it is a race. They go to great lengths to gain any advantage they can over others. For example, in the past, some have employed a shore-based weather expert to provide them with daily detailed meteorological advice to help them plan their routes. Another tactic has been to include a sailing tactician on the crew to develop a day-by-day, hour-by-hour sailing strategy to beat the opposition. This was the role that Sir Ben Ainslie fulfilled so successfully in the 2013 America's Cup competition.

If you were not one of the millions glued to the TV to watch that amazing race unfold, the climax involved two yachts going head to head, one representing the United States of America and the other, New Zealand. The first to reach 9 wins lifted the coveted cup. During the early stages, it was all going New Zealand's way. Team USA had to do something to change their fortunes and one of the things it did was to replace their tactician with Sir Ben. Despite being 8 to 1 down at one point, Team USA accomplished the most incredible comeback ever known, taking the trophy 9 to 8, with much of the credit going to Ben.

Those in the ARC Racing Division are single-minded; they want to win, and to win in a faster time than has been done before. But do not be fooled into thinking that these racers are all testosterone-fuelled macho men. One of the 2013 racing yachts had an all-female crew. The ladies wore crew T-shirts carrying the legend, 'Girls for Sail' written large across their backs, which grabbed people's attention as it was no doubt intended to do.

The 2013 rally

The 2013 ARC rally attracted more yachts than ever before. In fact, it was so heavily oversubscribed that the organisers laid on a separate rally for the overspill. In total, 221 yachts were accommodated in the conventional ARC rally, 35 of which were entered into the Racing Division and 24 in the Multihull Division. The other 162 made up the Cruising Division, including Second Wind. Although the racing yachts would start just a few minutes before the rest of us, it was likely that we would see only their rear ends, and those only for a short while as they disappeared into the distance, never to be seen again by the rest of the fleet until we reached the other side.

We on Second Wind had no illusions of taking on those racing boys (and girls). We knew the only way we could come first was if our yacht somehow got entangled with a passing whale who happened to winter in the West Indies and dragged us home with him. That was unlikely, although I would have enjoyed subsequently negotiating the film rights! For us four, the rally was first and foremost a challenge and we knew that we would feel immensely proud to achieve it, but secretly disappointed if we came in last, or arrived in Rodney Bay just as the bunting was being taken down.

Weather permitting, we would all set sail on the 24th November 2013. The rally is staged in November because, by then, the hurricane season should be over and helpful trade winds would normally be blowing to push the yachts across the ocean. Although the racers would be disappointed to take more than a fortnight for the crossing, our hope was to arrive during the second or third week of December, having taken advantage of those prevailing trade winds.

Second Wind described

Three years earlier, Chris had bought his yacht. No sooner had he seen a Moody 425 advertised for sale in Greece, he was on a plane, credit card in pocket. Like many weekend sailors, Chris had long dreamed of owning his own boat. In those dreams, he would buy a yacht and retire early to enjoy it. Then he woke up. Having bought the yacht, he had crossed that thin line between dreams and nightmares. The stark reality is that, generally speaking, having a boat also means having an income to keep it. So retiring was put on hold and his ongoing salary melted away each month in exchange for new sails, new rigging, new engine, and so on. The keel is original but Chris has renewed pretty much everything above it. We have all heard of the proverbial old broom that has only had five new broom-heads and six new handles in its long life. By the time of the rally, Second Wind was no different. Although officially manufactured in 1989, it was all but brand new.

For those interested in such things, the yacht is actually a sloop, having only a single mast. The mainsail is deployed by an in-mast furling system, which is great for adjusting the amount of sail to suit the wind, but is a serious pain in the neck should the sail become jammed, being almost impossible to free-up without conducting some serious surgery on the mast. The mainsail is supplemented by an expansive genoa headsail attached to the wire forestay that runs from the top of the mast to the bow. Two other sails are carried; a small but strong storm jib for heavy weather, and a huge but flimsy cruising chute for light winds.

All the winches are manual, requiring muscle power rather than electric power as and when sail adjustments are required. Helming is from a central cockpit, the helmsman protected at least partially by a perspex windshield. As money-buckets go, Second Wind is quite a weighty one for her 42 foot length. This makes it somewhat sluggish compared with the many lighter models, but does give greater stability and confidence in heavy seas.

Below deck, there are three places to sleep. The aft (back) cabin is commonly known as the owners' cabin, although there is nothing common about it. It is the largest and best appointed cabin by far, with a generous double bed set between a couch on one side and a dressing table and wardrobe on the other. If one had a ship's cat, this would be the only area below deck where you could swing it. Two doors lead off this cabin, one to an ensuite washroom cubicle and the other to a small cabin containing two bunks set hard up against the side of the boat.

While only a few inches from the owners' cabin in terms of distance, this twin bunk area is a million miles away in terms of luxury. Whereas the aft cabin is clearly designed for the complete comfort and convenience of the owners, the bunk section could well have been designed to accommodate an urchin or two who had just been press-ganged into service moments before sailing! The two bunks are enclosed on three sides and have minimal headroom, coffin-like in both their size and shape. Inserting yourself into one of these bunks is no easy task. Once in it, and having secured the canvas lee-cloth, shutting off the open side of the bunk to stop you rolling out in heavy seas, the coffin-like experience is complete.

In the bow of the boat is another cabin with a double bed of sorts. It is triangular in shape, following the contours of the hull. If used as a double, the users have to decide which parts of their anatomies they want forced together at the pointy end, either face to face, feet to feet, or face to feet! This decision normally depends on how well they know each other. Although bigger and more accessible than the bunks, the major disadvantage of using this bed on a voyage is that the bow of the boat rises up, crashes down and rolls around to a much greater extent than the stern, making it feel to the occupants more like a big-dipper than a bedroom.

Add to this the fact that the bed below you begins its crashing down while you, the occupant, are still on your way up, thus creating a void between man and mattress. Moments later, the two meet again, slammed together as the bed is on its way up and you are on your way down. Not much sleep is normally possible, but there is some consolation in knowing that people pay good money at Alton Towers for a few minutes of such an experience whereas this bed offers it the whole night long and for free.

This forward cabin has none of the soft furnishings or polished furniture enjoyed at the other end of the boat, although there is a door from it to the boat's second but smaller ensuite cubicle. Incidentally, when I speak of doors, please do not think of the doorways we have at home. Yacht doorways are an integral part of the general obstacle course that sailors endure daily. They are not wide enough for a grown man's shoulders to pass through broad ways and not high enough for a grown man's head to remain upright. Added to this, the opening does not extend all the way to the floor but has about a four inch lip to trip you. Thus, one does not simply walk through a doorway; it requires a contortion of the body such that you twist sideways from the hips up while, at the same time, ducking under the top and stepping over the lip.

For the most part, you come to perform this combination unconsciously as you move around the boat, but sooner or later there will be an occasion when you forget one of these three simultaneous movements. If you forget to twist, anything you happen to be carrying will be jolted from your hands and end up on the floor, butter-side down if it happens to be toast. If you forget to step, you will find yourself launched headlong at speed towards something that will break when you hit it in half-a-second or so, hurting yourself in the process. If you forget to duck, at best you will be rubbing a sore head while trying to suppress words that you should have left in the playground where you first heard them or, at worst, you will still be acting unconsciously, but this time for real rather than figuratively.

Between the fore and aft cabins is a good-sized saloon comprising a central table with upholstered bench seats either side of it, and an array of storage lockers behind, under and above these seats. Both of the washroom cubicles can also be accessed from this lounge area. At the aft end of this saloon on one side is a small but well-equipped galley, complete with a cooker comprising two burners, a grill and a small oven. Apart from the compass on deck, the cooker is the only other piece of equipment on gimbals, which should keep the pots and pans upright at sea, while everything else is at all sorts of angles, including the chef. There is also a small top-loaded fridge, but no freezer and certainly no watermaker. Washing up requires the pumping up of sea water into one of the two small sinks.

The chart table and all the ship's instruments are opposite the galley and, between the two, a seven-stepped, steep ladder gives access to the deck cockpit. These steps and access hatch are known as a companionway but are certainly not wide enough for companions to climb two abreast. The cockpit measures about seven feet by six feet and is dominated by the large helm wheel and a very useful fold-away table. The helm and the table are surrounded on three sides by hard bench seats.

Given that Second Wind is only about 12 feet across at its widest point, the skill of the designers has to be admired, squeezing so much in yet making her look good too. When new, she would certainly have been at the quality end of yachts, and although she is now getting on for a quarter of a century old, she has lasted well, her many polished mahogany surfaces showing few signs of age. There are certainly bigger and better boats about, but this one had all that was needed to carry us across an ocean.

What's in a name?

Second Wind was not always called Second Wind. When Chris bought her, she was called Laska II. Of all the many changes he has made to the yacht, changing her name was probably the least expensive. Dreaming up a new name is one of the few yachting dreams that comes almost free.

If you take a stroll around any harbour or marina, you will soon realise that boat owners can be very creative when it comes to christening their craft. There are countless names that are a play-on-nautical-words such as Nauti Bouy, Seas the Day, Lay A Wake, Devocean and Knot For Sail. Along the same lines, there are names that reflect the cost of boat ownership like Aquasition, Liquid Asset, In D Red, Myovadraft and best of all, A Crewed Interest.

There are thought-provoking names such as Unsinkable II. Or medical ones such as Cirrhosis Of The River and Vitamin Sea.

There are fishing-related names that may appeal to Robin, such as E-Fishient, O-Fish-L Business, Meals-on-Reels and Mullet Over. There are even Shakespearean names such as the one I borrowed for the title of this book, To Sea Oar Knot To Sea or, from slightly less highbrow literature, Miss Goody Two Screws. And there is my personal favourite, reminding us simply yet cleverly of all that separates the sailor from the seabed; Maid Of Plywood.

There are also plenty of extremely rude or risqué names, much better ignored, although it is perhaps worth mentioning that this has been so for centuries. The famous tea clipper, Cutty Sark, somehow seems less of a grand old lady of the sea when you learn that her Scottish name means 'Skimpy Underskirt'. This was captured well by Robert Burns in his erotic Tam o'Shanta poem of 1791, part of which reads:

Her cutty sark, o' Paisley harn,
That while a lassie she had worn,
In longitude tho' sorely scanty,
It was her best, and she was vauntie.

It may help to know that 'vauntie' means joyously proud, and Chris was therefore vauntie when, having pondered many options, he finally settled on the name, Second Wind. He had been influenced in part by the name, Seventh Wave, which belongs to a splendid 49 foot Hallberg-Rassy on which the two of us, with other friends, once sailed together around some of Scotland's stunningly beautiful islands and inlets.

With that sense of satisfied smugness that often accompanies original thought, Chris made all the name-change arrangements, applied the lettering transfers to the hull and the deed was done. It was some time later that Glyn, who had read up on such matters, showed him an article pointing out that Second Wind routinely ranked in the Top Ten of the most common boat names. There are hundreds of them! I had thought naïvely that, should the worst happen mid-Atlantic, I could put out a Mayday and simply say, "You cannot miss us, we are the white yacht called Second Wind." Now I knew that was akin to saying, "I am in the telephone directory under Smith."

Moreover, here is a strange fact. Say to anyone that you have changed the name of a boat and they will tell you that they thought it was an unlucky thing to do. And I mean anyone, not just people connected with the sea. Try it for yourself. If you do not have a yacht, pretend that you do (the cheapest way of owning a boat). Then mention to the check-out girl at the supermarket, or the postman, or to Great Aunt Agatha when she comes to tea, that you are thinking of changing its name, and they will tell you that they read something or saw somewhere that it was an unlucky thing to do! And this belief is not confined to modern times. In the classic novel, Treasure Island, the infamous Long John Silver said:

"That was Roberts' men, that was, and comed of changing names to their ships – Royal Fortune and so on. Now, what a ship was christened, so let her stay, I says."

By these words, the one-legged scoundrel was asserting that his pirate friends had been hanged and 'sun-dried', not because they had been caught, tried and found guilty of heinous crimes but solely because they had re-named their ships. Remarkably, author Robert Louis Stevenson was weaving his tales of treasure and treachery in the 1880s so it was clearly deemed unlucky to change a vessel's name way back then just as it is now.

But we do not believe in luck. Second Wind it is and Atlantic Ocean here we come!

A novice's view of things so far

Knowing that I had not undertaken any formal sail-training, my daughter had bought me a copy of the Royal Yachting Association's Day Skipper Handbook, which I read right through to help prepare myself for the ARC rally. Additionally, I booked another sailing holiday in Scotland on the yacht, Seventh Wave. The book was theoretical and the holiday practical, but both proved instructive. I was, however, left pondering two big questions.

The first was this: Given that the BBC reported in early 2013 that the Castle View School in Essex had banned triangular-shaped flapjacks after a pupil was injured when one had been flung at him, where on earth was Health & Safety hiding when yachting was on the agenda?

I appreciate that for some, the deck of a yacht is no more than a place to support a sunbed and rest a gin & tonic as the docile waters of some tranquil sea or marina, gently lap and slap around them. But when it comes to any serious sailing, the deck is a place of work, and a more hazardous one it is hard to imagine. Taking Second Wind as an example, her slender deck measures only about 250 square feet. That is roughly equivalent to the surface area of just five table-tennis tables, and yet the deck has four different levels, none of them level, and they merge into each other by slippery slopes of varying degrees of slant.

Scattered across this undulating deck space is every

conceivable trip-hazard. These include five glass-topped hatches that each protrude about two inches from the deck surface, four vent apertures, five rail-like pieces of equipment, four winches and two contraptions that look so like the tubular walking frames used by the elderly that they are actually called, granny bars.

Taking up much of the little left-over space are two large bags strapped to the deck, one containing the cruising chute – the sail for use in lighter winds – and the other holding the deflated rubber dinghy. Also strapped down at the point of the bow is a large box containing a petrol-driven generator and three fuel cans to feed it. With eyes down, looking to avoid these trip hazards, one runs the risk of being snared by any of the ten wire shrouds that secure the mast, or indeed, by the mast itself, with its own array of gadgets and hooks, all designed to snag the unsuspecting sailor. Now throw in an abundance of ropes, high and low, long and short, loose and taut, and you have the makings of an assault course fit for the finest commando.

Finally, if all of that does not get you, there is always the boom. Hinged at the mast, and weighing the equivalent of many tons when the mainsail is filled with wind, this fifteen-foot metal contraption can sweep across the boat with ferocious power, and will in a moment skittle anything or anyone in its way. Joking apart, it is a potential killer. Many a human nut has been cracked wide open by a speeding but silent boom.

If all that was not enough to give your average Health & Safety rep heart failure several times over, one takes this deck with all its hazards, and places it on the most unstable base known to man – water – and then throws in wind, waves and currents to make sure nothing stands still, even for a moment! Who knows, the Castle View School may well have potentially saved the lives of countless kids by their insistence that flapjacks should only be of the less-lethal oblong variety, but compared with yachting, I think I would rather take my chances with a flying triangular treat, however dangerous they are.

The other big question I pondered was why sailors down through the ages saw the need for inventing new words when there were perfectly good ones already available to describe most things. Glyn first alerted me to this. As I mentioned, at one of our planning meetings, he had volunteered to look after the listing and buying of our food and drink for the voyage, but his actual words were, "Put me down with victualling." To me, this sounded more like the last request of a terminally-ill dog pleading with its owner.

I soon realised that those who sail have to first master a whole new vocabulary that has its roots in antiquity. For example, you do not get on a boat but rather you 'climb a-board', harking back to when the side of a boat was called a board. Hence, when you fall off it, having tripped on one of the many previously-mentioned deck hazards, you are 'over board'. Speed is still measured in knots and recorded in logs from the days when throwing a log attached to a knotted string over the board was the only way to measure how fast you were travelling, or indeed, whether you were moving at all.

Even simple things are not as simple as they first appear. Why, for example, is a quarterdeck not a quarter of a deck? Or to take another example, we probably all know, in marine-speak, that left becomes port and right becomes starboard. But watch any old pirate film, or even the frantic bridge scene of the blockbuster Titanic movie as the iceberg is suddenly sighted, and sooner or later someone will yell to the helmsman, "Hard a-starboard!" by which they meant, "Steer to port." Clear as mud!

Or what about sails and ropes? To the uninitiated, sails look like bed sheets but are not called sheets, whereas the ropes that control the sails look nothing like sheets, yet that is exactly what they are called. By the same reasoning I suppose, a rope attached to a life-raft is called a painter, presumably because it looks nothing like, well, a painter.

It gets worse. Sometimes it depends where you are on the boat as to what you call something. For instance, the top of the saloon is called a coach roof when standing above it but a deckhead when standing below it. Perhaps a better example is that, above deck, 'ahead full' means go as fast as you can whereas, below deck, 'a head full' means you need to get your rubber gloves on. That is because, above deck, ahead relates to forward motion whereas, below deck, a head relates to bowel motion. No-one will thank you for getting that mixed up, although I do not believe that such a confusion led to the term 'poop deck'.

Inadvertently, learning this new vocabulary made me realise that the distance across the Atlantic Ocean was longer than I had first thought. I had not banked on nautical miles being longer than conventional miles. The 2,800 nautical miles that I had signed up for actually equates to about 3,200 conventional miles. So the challenge was growing even before we had started. And we were far from ready and Second Wind was far from the rally start-line; she needed to be in Gran Canaria but she was in Gibraltar, about 900 nautical miles, or 1,000 real ones, from the Canaries. Fortunately, we had best part of a year to sail her there.

Chapter Two

A little training and a lot of planning

Three days, three courses

One of the sensible ARC rally guidelines is that the skipper and one other of the crew should have completed courses in Offshore Safety, Sea Survival and First Aid. The Royal Yachting Association combines these courses, running them over three consecutive days, one day for each topic. We decided that it would be both beneficial and bonding for us all to enlist and attend the RYA course together. All too soon, the time for the training came around. It was the first week of March 2013 when we travelled together to Hamble on the Solent, all a little apprehensive as to what might lay ahead.

In some respects our apprehension was well founded. We reflected afterwards that the Offshore Safety course could easily be called 'You're Going To Die', Sea Survival renamed, 'You're Going To Die Slowly' and First Aid called 'You're Going To Die Slowly But Well-Bandaged'. All three days were punctuated with images of holed yachts, dismasted yachts and upside-down yachts, all accompanied by grim facts and figures about death and drowning, distress and destruction.

Not only that, but those seafaring disaster stories seemed to stimulate the course attendees into chipping in with their own yarns of marine mayhem. Not to be outdone, Chris recalled the time when one of his crew had to be airlifted to hospital after a freak accident involving a spinnaker pole falling from the mast and embedding itself in the unfortunate man's head. It must have been quite a memorable experience, except for the casualty who could be forgiven for not remembering a thing.

Ron was our tutor for Offshore Safety and he was clearly a man of vast experience. Unnervingly, he warned that even safety equipment could sometimes become the enemy in stormy seas, regaling us with stories of jackstays coming unfastened and flinging the attached sailor into the sea, a helmsman being washed off the stern of his yacht as his safety line was attached too far back, and a skipper who was working near the bow of his boat and whose safety line, rather than saving him, actually secured him underwater as his yacht heeled over. Ron had our rapt attention!

Part of the first day was spent on a pontoon in the marina. There we got to rehearse different methods of recovering a body from the water. This gave us helpful insight into the type of recovery equipment we might need for the Atlantic crossing. Inadvertently, it also gave us a warning about the effects of hypothermia - it was perishing cold on that pontoon, yet as we shivered, we learned that our body warmth would have leeched away well over 20 times faster, had we been in the water rather than just standing next to it.

The chilly pontoon experience was followed by a practical session on the use and misuse of flares. That warmed us up, some more than others. One of our fellow classmates learned the hard way to ensure the flare is the right way up before holding it out at arm's length. If not, the flame travels quickly up your sleeve and removes your armpit hair quicker than any cosmetic waxing. Ouch!

My lesson was not to look directly at the flame of the flare if you want to be able to see anything else for the next ten minutes or so. And taking those few extra seconds to put on gloves before firing flares came to the rescue of Chris. The telescopic part of the hand-held flare he was firing failed, the burning end sliding back into the handle he was holding, catching it alight. Had he not put the gloves on, it would have certainly burned his hands. We quickly switched our attention from testing flares to testing fire extinguishers, and the burning handle incident was dealt with in an instant.

Finally, a couple of tips for everyone. Always stand downwind of those orange smoke flares; if you do not, when the smoke ceases, your expensive Henri Lloyd sailing jacket will be orange, and will remain so for evermore. And the other tip? If you, like us, are the wrong side of fifty, it would be wise to keep a cheap pair of reading glasses in your flare box. The yachting mantra concerning flares is 'Read Before You Need' but, as we get older, our memories as well as our eyesight fails us, so having those cheap glasses to hand could help save your life or, at the very least, your armpit.

"Personally I am always willing to learn, although I do not always like being taught." (Sir Winston Churchill)

The second course was Sea Survival and could not have been more different. Just as our day-one tutor was a man of vast experience, our main day-two tutor was a man of vast waistline. He came with a much smaller-proportioned assistant, and the two interacted like a modern-day Laurel & Hardy. The major tutor, like Hardy, was clearly an important man in his own mind, overbearing in manner and bullying the mild-mannered minor tutor who responded, Laurel-like, with barely audible murmurings. Had we really paid good money for this? Like Churchill before us, we did not like the way we were being taught but we decided to set that aside, still willing to learn all we could from the course content.

As things turned out, the course proved very useful, especially the practical session in the local swimming pool. That gave us invaluable firsthand experience of swimming fully clothed in a lifejacket, deploying and entering a life-raft, and righting a raft that had been overturned. We all had to do this righting of a raft individually. The procedure involved pulling the life-raft over, allowing it to flop down on top of us, such that we were then beneath it. That created an air-pocket above our head. Counter-intuitively, we had to pause and take a breath from that air-pocket before swimming out from under the raft.

It was during that exercise that the real stature of minor-tutor emerged. He was in the water with each of us, waiting for us as we surfaced into the air-pocket. There, his quiet words were clearly audible, telling us not to worry, that he was with us and was not going to leave us, and how well we were doing. Despite the differences in physique between major and minor tutors, the latter proved himself a giant of a man in comparison.

Perhaps more so than my crewmates, I had been very apprehensive about the pool exercise. As I had stood on the pool-side, ready to simulate 'abandon ship', memories flooded back of a time when I was standing on the edge of a yacht my brother and Robin had chartered in the Solent. We had enjoyed a great sail around the Isle of Wight in cold and choppy conditions, and now we were in the marina heading for an empty pontoon. Standing the wrong side of the guardrail, bowline in hand, I was leaning away from the yacht, readying myself to step onto the pontoon as soon as it became in reach. But before 'in reach' was reached, I felt my grip fail me and, in an instant, I was in the water; just me and the half-dozen layers of clothing I was wearing against the cold, topped off with foul weather gear and a lifejacket.

I doggy-paddled to the pontoon's edge with ease but, despite the added incentive of knowing that a 40 foot yacht was bearing down on me, eager to share the same pontoon space, there was no way on this earth that I could lift myself out of the water. Every layer of clothing had trapped what felt like gallons of water, making me look and feel like the Michelin Man. A kind soul working on his boat nearby ran to my rescue and hauled me clear. I was safe, and so was my brother's non-returnable deposit against loss or damage. We were both happy. It was from that incident that Chris began to refer to me as 'Fenders' as they too drop over the sides of boats.

Tales of the sea

As the second day of training concluded, despite not warming to the training style, we all recognised that we had enjoyed a lot of good learning and a lot of good laughing too. We laughed, for example, on being told that, in a survival situation, we should only throw someone from the life-raft back into the sea when they began to smell. We agreed they probably meant that, in addition to smelling, they also showed no signs of life. I do not think they were giving us carte blanche to eject a crew member simply because of his body odour.

There was something else that raised a smile, if a grimace can be called a smile. It was the true-life story of Dougal and

Lyn Robertson and their family who had to take to their life-raft after their yacht was struck by a pod of killer whales. Their remarkable story is told in the book, Survive the Savage Sea. They endured 37 days adrift and only survived because, among other things, Lyn repeatedly administered rainwater enemas to everyone. The rainwater would have been fatally poisonous to drink as it was contaminated with salt, turtle blood and offal. Those enemas proved the only effective way of keeping their bodies hydrated without the fatal risks associated with drinking the noxious solution. Like most people on hearing about the enema nightmare, I had laughed and clenched simultaneously.

My three crewmates, however, were quicker to see that the ability to administer such enemas could be a life-saver and they were later discussing seriously whether a length of garden hose would suffice, or whether more slender tubing would be less eye-wateringly severe on the tender rectal membrane. Chris subsequently worked out how a hand-held water pump could be adapted to do the business. From listening to those discussions, I knew that Second Wind's survival Grab Bag would be augmented to include all we needed for such administrations. Can't wait.

Another of our tutor's stories was of three people surviving a long period at sea on the upturned hull of their boat. They had apparently told accident investigators that they survived by eating fish, birds and turtles, whereas the truth slowly emerged that there had originally been four people on the hull! Urban myth or not, I was pleased that my three sailing buddies had not started planning for that eventuality too, although Chris & Chips has a nice ring to it. That would teach him for calling me Fenders!

Reflections in the pool

The pool exercises brought home some key learning points very powerfully. So much so that, although I do not pretend to be an expert of any sort, even I would urge anyone without a moment's hesitation to do two things: First, if your lifejacket does not have crutch straps, fit them. The buoyancy aids we used in the pool did not have these straps, deliberately so, to make us realise just how much lifejackets tend to ride up in water. In the pool, one of our hands was almost permanently occupied with trying to pull the buoyancy aid back down to where it should have been, and in a life or death situation, both hands are needed for other things.

Secondly, if your spray hood is not attached to the collar of your lifejacket, get one that is. Some hoods are housed in a little pocket on one of the lifejacket straps. It may look neat and tidy but again, in cold and choppy water, getting the hood out, working out how it fits, and then fitting it, takes time that one simply does not have. For the ARC rally, Chris had bought crutch straps for all four lifejackets and fitted spray hoods to their collars. The rest of us were reassured by his foresight.

However, not having a spray hood at all, or not being able to deploy it, does have one somewhat spurious advantage; it could prevent death by hypothermia. On the face of it, this sounds like good news, as hypothermia is anything but pleasant. First our bodies have to deal with the shock of sudden immersion in cold water. That in itself can trigger cardiac arrest or a stroke from our hearts pumping madly and our blood pressure rising dramatically. If we survive that, then cramps and nausea set in as our heart rate falls. Then our breathing becomes ever more laboured and our strength ebbs away, leaving us unable to swim or even wave goodbye as we slip into unconsciousness.

The lack of a spray hood may prevent this horror but only because we would die from the greater horror of drowning long before hypothermia had time to do its worst. Without a spray hood, sea water would flow into us. This is unstoppable because our breathing, coughing and swallowing mechanisms are all automatically put on hold by bodies trying to fight the greater enemy of cold. It surprised us to learn that just one-and-a-half litres of water swallowed inadvertently and sloshing around our lungs would be enough to end a man.

If it is any consolation, we were told the following simple way to at least make our bodies immune to cold water shock; when taking a hot shower in the days and weeks leading up to a voyage, just turn the water temperature down to cold for a couple of minutes before getting out. Instinctively this made sense and I believed it, but I knew in my heart that I was not going to try it.

I was left musing how Second Wind's crew would work together should one of us ever become hypothermic. Gentle warming is apparently the order of the day. On learning that this would include undressing the casualty and then redressing him, cuddling him to share bodily warmth and perhaps sharing a sleeping bag for the same reason, the notion of 'working together' soon evaporated and 'every man for himself' took on renewed appeal.

All of this invaluable medical information was gained at our third day First Aid course, expertly presented by Sue, our tutor for that day. Sue was able to combine her extensive knowledge of all things gory with an equally extensive knowledge of life aboard a boat. Robin in particular, as our resident fisherman, winced when she told of fish-hooks being caught in eyelids. And I am certain that none of us would ever be found cooking chilli in our underpants after Sue described the scalding incurred when somebody did just that. For clarity, I think the casualty was cooking chilli in the galley while wearing his underpants rather than cooking the chilli *in* his underpants.

I imagined for a brief moment (excuse the pun) that it had been one of us who had suffered the underpants incident and wondered about my brother's reaction to any of us wanting to run fresh cold water over our scalded parts. At sea, fresh water is more precious than rubies. Would he permit us to drain his freshwater tank simply to relieve our agony? Or would he expect us to do the decent thing, follow the example of Captain Oates and walk off the back of the boat echoing his immortal words, "I may be gone some time." I hoped we would never find out.

As a result of Sue's compelling tuition, our onboard first aid kit would soon be augmented with spray-on plaster, wide steri-strips, haemostatic granules, paraffin gauze and cetrimide-infused anti-bacterial washes, not to mention a magnet for extracting metal fragments from eyeballs and tampons for staunching nosebleeds (although not those with the plastic applicators). Why so relaxed over such expenditure? It is because accidents or injuries that would merely be inconvenient ashore can be fatal at sea. First Aid is normally temporary until Second Aid arrives. But when there is no Second Aid coming...? Funny how that concentrated our minds and opened our wallets!

However comprehensive our first aid kit would be, it could

never replace the remarkable remedies that our bodies produce without our intervention. It was fascinating to learn and appreciate how ingeniously the human body reacts to threat or peril. Without any conscious command from us, blood, air and hormones are instantly dispatched to wherever they are most needed to protect our vital organs and sustain life amid the gravest of dangers. We are all walking works of art, wonderfully put together.

Our three days together had more than met our expectations and certainly heightened our awareness of many things. As the saying goes, 'better a thousand times careful than once dead'. None of us became an overnight expert in anything, but we had come away knowing that we would all be taking that extra care in trying to avoid the first aid kit ever being opened, the life-raft ever being deployed, or crepitus – the sound of fractured bones rubbing together – ever being heard. The only cry we wanted to hear was that of the gulls!

As we drove home from the Solent, our previous apprehensions about the course had been replaced with new apprehensions about the numerous ocean-sailing threats highlighted by our tutors. At least we now knew about them and felt better prepared to face them. And we all had certificates to prove it.

Three part planning

Planning for us had three component parts. One was social, and Glyn became expert in organising a fair few curry nights just so that we could get to know one-another better. That was not as easy as it sounds. Attempting to find mutually convenient dates in the diaries of four busy men was like trying to shepherd cats, so Glyn's persistence and perseverance was appreciated. Apart from comparing different Indian restaurants, those evenings were also useful for determining how hot we should make our curries when afloat. It became clear that Robin preferred cool kormas, I liked fiery phals, and Chris and Glyn were somewhere in between.

"The planning stage of a cruise is often just as enjoyable as the voyage itself, letting one's imagination loose on all kinds of possibilities. Yet translating dreams into reality means a lot of practical questions have to be answered." (Jimmy Cornell - World Cruising Handbook)

The second part of our planning was getting together for several formal meetings to work our way through an agenda while also working our way through home-baked pizzas. Jimmy Cornell knew what he was talking about. It was he who organised the very first ARC rally in 1986 and subsequently founded the World Cruising Club. He said planning was enjoyable and it was. As we let our imaginations range over a raft of possibilities, the practical questions emerged.

It was at our planning meetings that we focused in on the many decisions that had to be made about watch systems, storage, safety, insurance, fishing, clothing, medical supplies and a hundred and one other things, but mainly food – how much of it we needed, where we were going to buy it, how we were going to keep it, and who was going to cook it. None of us professed to be a chef but we were encouraged by Chris who said of cooking, "How hard can it be? Even women do it." I am sure Chris thinks he probably got away with that comment, but when his wife Angela reads this book, as I am certain she will, I think he may pay for it yet.

The third element of our planning was easily the best part; the hands-on, practical part. In May 2013, we all flew out to Gibraltar to work on the boat for about a week. Coincidentally, as we took off from Gatwick Airport, cities across the UK were hosting events to commemorate the 70th anniversary of the Battle of the Atlantic. Here we were, flying out of the country to prepare Second Wind for her own Atlantic battle, hopefully nowhere near as dangerous.

Working together

There was a lot to do. First, Second Wind had to be emptied of numerous non-essential items to make room for all the extra equipment and supplies that we would have to carry. Much was thrown away or, if too good for that, stuffed into suitcases to make the return journey home with us. Next, additional storage had to be created, as cruising yachts are not designed to accommodate self-sufficient living over a lengthy period of time. Chris fixed two capacious hammock-like nets from the roof of the saloon and we began to fill them with tins of food. Frequently forgetting they were there, we each of us clouted our heads on the tins enough times to convince us that we needed to find a better place to stow them.

This was more important than it may sound. During our Offshore Safety course, we had been told of one skipper who, in a violent storm, was rendered unconscious by a flying tin of baked beans. We had already accumulated over 100 tins of food for our ARC voyage, and we probably needed at least 100 more. Anyone sharing a berth with those on a dark and stormy night ran the risk of coming to a very sticky end in the midst of something akin to an artillery barrage of tinned treacle puddings and the like. I was not sure Maureen would ever live it down if my Death Certificate cited 'Death by Peaches' as the cause of my premature demise. We decided that the safest thing to do was to restrict ourselves to one loo and transform the other loo-cubicle into a larder. At a stroke, our decision solved our storage dilemma as well as ensuring that the mortal danger of a tin bombardment was contained.

"Behold also the ships, which though they be so great, and are driven of fierce winds, yet are they turned about with a very small helm, withersoever the governor listeth." (Bible: James 3:4)

Finding and renovating Second Wind's emergency tiller was another of the many jobs we had to do to prepare the yacht for action. That vital piece of equipment would allow us to still move the rudder should the helm mechanism fail. Although the rudder of a boat is one of the smallest bits, it does one of the biggest jobs. If we lost the ability to turn the rudder, then Second Wind could not have been steered, and that could have disastrous consequences.

Those of us old enough to have an interest in the Second World War will know that the pride of the German fleet was the battleship, Bismarck. Although Bismarck positively bristled with powerful guns and state-of-the-art equipment, she was rendered impotent when her rudder was jammed, following a torpedo strike. Despite all the ingenuity of her design, the great ship could do nothing except go round in circles while frantic hands struggled to repair the damage and restore her steering. But it all took too long and, in the meantime, Bismarck became a sitting duck for the lesser guns of pursuing British Navy ships. Having sustained fatal damage, she was scuttled by her crew and went to the seabed taking many brave men with her. And all because of a jammed rudder.

The idea of going round in circles mid-Atlantic appeals to no-one. To help prevent that happening, the World Cruising Club lays down that all boats sailing the ARC rally must carry emergency steering equipment. Second Wind's emergency tiller is a four foot length of heavy-duty tubular steel with a short fixing rod protruding at one end, which slots into a socket at the rear of the deck. But because it is one of those bits of kit that is almost never used, ours was rusty, wrapped in plastic bags, stowed at the bottom of a deep deck locker and all but forgotten. Having located it, we set about smartening it up.

This brings me to offering another tip. Never stow anything you may not need for a long time in bio-degradable plastic bags. As they degrade, they metamorphise from a single sheet of plastic into thousands of tiny plastic shreds, each one with the ability to stick like superglue to whatever it was meant to protect. That is what had happened to the plastic bags that once wrapped the emergency tiller. Trying to pick off those shreds merely transferred them to our fingers and then onto anything else we picked up to help us in the task. After each shred of plastic had eventually been removed, Robin de-rusted and cleaned the tiller, and I painted it bright red to make it easier to spot in its deep dark home. Convinced that our emergency tiller must now be the cleanest in the fleet, we returned it to the deck locker but, this time, without its plastic-bag covering.

We continued to work our way through a lengthy list of things to be done, such as erecting a frame to hold the two solar panels, installing the required 'single side-band radio' and hoisting its aerial to the top of the mast, resurrecting an ancient petrol-driven generator to power our fridge, netting off large gaps under the guardrails to prevent losing things to the sea in heavy swells, inserting a safety switch into the gas system, and many other things besides. Working together each day was a pleasure, but whiling away the evenings together was even better.

I had never before fully understood why so many yachts are never ventured beyond their harbour walls. A huge number spend all of their days tied to a marina pontoon and hosting only occasional visits from their owners, who use them just as floating picnic tables, albeit very expensive floating picnic tables. But during those evenings together in Gibraltar, I was beginning to get it. There was something very special about relaxing on the yacht's deck in twilight warmth, being gently rocked by nearly still waters and lulled by the soothing sounds that only halyards and masts can make together. It was almost entrancing to watch the sun set and the moon rise from the comfort of cushions in the cockpit, illuminated by just a candle lantern. It was more than pleasant to recline and enjoy good cheese, good wine, good company and good conversation as the gulls circled overhead, their white undersides appearing incandescent as they reflected the harbour lights.

Sometimes we laid back and listened to music long into the night, or Robin would play the boat's guitar, his nimble fingers playfully scaling its fretboard while Chris accompanied on his harmonicas. Other times, we just chatted, putting the world to rights and sharing stories and memories. At one point, Chris and I reminisced about the first time we ever sailed together, remembering back to when we were small children. It was on a boating lake in Dorset's Poole Park, in a little wooden dinghy that our dad had hired for an hour or so. How we wished our parents were still alive to see us these years later, although both would have been upset. Mum would have been upset with worry over what we were doing. In fact, had she been alive, it would have killed her. Dad would have been upset that he was not going with us. If he had been alive but not invited, it would have killed him; any adventurous streak in us came from him and he would have been thrilled to share in our adventure.

When our conversation moved onto music, as it invariably did, Glyn and Robin took centre stage and more than impressed Chris and me with their deep and wide knowledge of past and present bands, music in general, musicians in particular and concerts through the ages. Adding immensely to our joy was great news from home. Robin's two sons are themselves talented musicians and together they compose and perform computer-generated electronic dance music. The news was that they were riding high in the national music charts, having been catapulted over recent weeks from relative obscurity to the bright limelight of fame.

The brothers perform under the name, Disclosure. If you are anything like our age, that name will probably mean nothing to you, but if you are 40 years younger, it may well make you swoon or go weak at the knees. Robin's pride in his sons overflowed to the rest of us and we all basked in their reflected glory. Well done lads! What a perfect way to end a busy day.

Monkey business

In the daylight hours, we allowed ourselves a little time to explore the sights of Gibraltar. A little time was all we needed. The tiny British Overseas Territory covers not much more than two square miles of soil and limestone, yet has been besieged and attacked many times over, not because of its size but because of its enviable strategic position, commanding the entrance to the Mediterranean. Having strolled its one main street and sampled coffee in its one main square, we took the cable car up to the top of the Rock which dominates Gibraltar and which, down through the centuries, has enabled it to repel all those who have attempted to take it by force.

Today, that same Rock is better known for being home to some 300 monkeys, or Barbary Macaques, argued to now be Gibraltar's main tourist attraction. We could not leave without seeing them. We watched as they scaled the buildings and scavenged for food. Heavy fines awaited anyone who fed them, but that did not deter these enterprising apes from stealing food from unsuspecting tourists and then vaulting over the roofs of cars to prevent them giving chase; a sight that was well worth seeing.

How those North African monkeys came to be in Gibraltar has long been lost in the mists of time, but legend maintains that they found their way through a subterranean tunnel that once supposedly linked the Rock to Morocco, some 15 miles distant, and separated by the choppy waters of the Strait of Gibraltar. If that legend explains their arrival, another legend explains why they are still around. The latter legend holds that Gibraltar would remain under British rule only while the monkeys remained in residence.

This may not be believed by everyone but wartime Prime Minister, Sir Winston Churchill took no chances and, in 1942, he ordered that the seven remaining monkeys be brought some new friends from Morocco and Algeria. They obviously liked their new friends and their numbers quickly swelled. No-one can be certain what part if any the monkeys played, but what is certain is that the several subsequent attacks by German, Italian and Vichy French forces during the Second World War all came to nothing. Clever monkeys!

Once down at sea level again, Robin persuaded us to stay a while in a tavern that was hosting an 'open mic' night. It is no exaggeration to say that the crew of Second Wind made up the entire audience at one point that evening, the quality of the 'music' having something to do with it. But showbiz is in Robin's blood, and we could see him itching and twitching to borrow a guitar and belt out a song. Now it was our turn to persuade him, and so we left, keeping his talents under wraps until another time.

On our way back to the marina, I happened to notice an Insurance Broker's window and was somewhat taken aback by the words stencilled on it. I had seen many similar windows in the UK, listing as they do all the things that insurance policies cover, such as Aviation, Healthcare, Travel, and so on. But the final cover listed on this particular window sent a sudden shiver down my spine; 'Kidnap & Ransom' – a reminder to me of just how close we were to Africa and its pirate problems. I wondered how much my wife might part with for my safe return!

All too soon, it was time for us to make that safe return to England, our budget airliner touching down on the tarmac of Gatwick Airport. Our plan was to return to Gibraltar in

June, but then we would only need a one-way ticket as we would be sailing Second Wind those 900 nautical miles to the ARC start line in Gran Canaria. But before that, we had an immediate little challenge to overcome. Remember me saying about stuffing suitcases with random stuff that we did not need on the boat but was too good to throw away? Well, one of the cases we used was an ancient Samsonite that had done faithful service not only to us but to our parents before us. It was the old rigid variety, the two halves held together by twin locks.

Unfortunately, despite what I am sure was the gentlest of handling for which Gatwick baggage handlers are renowned, our sturdy suitcase somehow exploded open just as it was ejected onto the baggage carousel. It was like a scene from the Generation Game, with our now open and empty case followed by a trail of old paint brushes and roller-trays, lengths of copper tubing and electrical cable, a half-used block of cheese, a baking tray past its prime, a piece of chorizo sausage, offcuts of sail canvas and numerous other bits of sailing paraphernalia. We casually retrieved our goods as if no-one was watching or laughing and went on our way, making a mental note to buy a strap for the Samsonite suitcase which, we were sure, had years of life left in it yet.

Back to Gibraltar

June came, and we were back at the Queensway Quay marina in Gibraltar, temporary home to Second Wind since September 2012. It was interesting to observe the different priorities of my sailing buddies on boarding the yacht again after an absence. Chris immediately checked the bilges to see if there was any ingress of water. Robin immediately checked the guitar to see if it was still in tune. Glyn immediately checked the clock to see whether it was one of his 'phone home' slots allocated to him by his wife, Thelma. Glyn's sailing gear may have been with him on the boat but it was clear who wore the salopettes at home! As for me, I was still not knowledgeable enough to check anything so I reverted to type and, being English, made us all a cup of tea.

We had allowed ourselves a few days at the marina before setting sail for Gran Canaria, not least because Chris had organised delivery of a new life-raft, suitably rated for ocean crossing, to replace his lower-rated but otherwise perfectly good raft. That purchase represented the biggest expenditure in our ARC preparations, yet was one of those rare investments that we hoped would never prove its worth. Getting it aboard was far from easy. The raft was very heavy and cumbersome, its rigid outer case constructed without hand-holds. We had to man-handle the thing across a less-than-stable gangplank only about twelve inches wide, and then lift it up and over the yacht's rear guardrails. The wise seafaring adage of 'always keep one hand for the boat and one hand for yourself' was impossible to follow as three of us struggled and stumbled with our heavy load.

As we had wobbled our way across the gangplank, some morbid statistics came to mind; I had read that eight out of ten sailors who die, do so from drowning but, incredibly, about six of those eight would not be sailing at the time! It was hard to conceive that the relatively calm and shallow waters of harbours and marinas could claim more lives than the open seas, but we were in danger of proving the fact. The three of us could easily have lost our precarious balance and toppled into the water, ironically with a brand new life-raft within reach but as useful as a chocolate teapot.

Eventually we succeeded in our struggle, and the new raft was rested on Second Wind's rear deck while we took a moment for our breathing patterns to return to something near normal. It was only then that we noticed the raft casing was not properly sealed at one corner. How could something so costly have been allowed to leave the factory so obviously faulty?

Frantic phone calls followed, resulting in a specialist engineer coming aboard to try to repack and reseal the raft. He wrestled with the problem for some considerable time before admitting defeat and telling us that the raft would have to be returned to the manufacturer. This was no good to us as we were sailing away in a day or so. The chandlers who had sold Chris the faulty raft had only one other ocean-rated model in stock, costing a few hundred pounds more than the one he had bought. But given the urgency of our circumstances, we took it, and twice more pitted our wits against the narrow gangplank and awkward railings as we manoeuvred the faulty raft off, and the new one on to Second Wind.

We used our final day in Gibraltar to buy the perishable foodstuffs that we needed for the journey south. Glyn would have us believe that victualling is a noble art but in reality, it just meant repeatedly walking the mile or so to the nearest supermarket and, dare I admit to it, walking back pulling one of those 'granny' shopping baskets on wheels that most men inwardly vow never to do. Chris knew this was potentially embarrassing and took great pleasure in capturing it all on his iPhone video, no doubt for some future blackmailing scam.

On the food front, we made a last minute change to our plan.

Working on a boat moored further down our pontoon was a man who, with his wife, had sailed more ocean miles than we had had hot dinners. He advised us that hot dinners was what we needed and urged us to prepare a few in advance of our voyage. We took his advice, not knowing how grateful we would later be. So in the relative calm of the marina, I knocked up a couple of hot chilli meals, but I did it carefully, still mindful of the underpants incident.

As a new day dawned, the forecast being favourable, we were ready to embark on the longest sail by far that any of us had experienced, and this one without the support of the World Cruising Club. We were on our own. We had decided to break the journey, heading first for the island of Madeira, and then south from there to Gran Canaria. Sharing the voyage with us was a mutual friend, Ian, as keen as we were for the experience. Having Ian with us was a real bonus; amiable and easygoing by nature, and with knowledge and skills to supplement our own. But he also brought to the table, quite literally, something that could make a grown man drool - the recipe and ingredients for his wife's famously-delicious cashew-nut paella. It was clear that we were going to eat very well. I found myself reconsidering that weight gain, weight loss question.

Chapter Three

Gran Canaria, here we come

From cloud to cloud

"I wandered lonely as a cloud that floats on high o'er vales and hills." (William Wordsworth)

I used to think that William Wordsworth knew nothing about clouds. My response to his famous lines was that he obviously did not live where I do. Where I live, clouds are never lonely. They are more like the sorrows of Shakespeare's Hamlet, coming 'not as single spies but in battalions'. I have often seen cloudless skies, and I have often seen cloud-filled skies, but just one lonely cloud in an otherwise sky of blue is as rare as hen's teeth. Until, that is, we got to know Gibraltar.

The famous Rock of Gibraltar towers nearly 1,400 feet above the marina where Second Wind was moored, but towering for another 150 feet or so above that was a single solitary cloud that seemed somehow glued to the Rock top. All around it, the sky was blue. If we looked to the north, the sun was shining there. If we looked the other way, it was shining there too. In fact, the sun seemed to shine everywhere except in the shadow of the Rock itself. Day after day, as we had busied ourselves preparing the yacht for sail, that single cloud had been our constant canopy.

To blame was something called the levanter wind. It is a moist, easterly wind that streams close to the sea's surface through the Strait of Gibraltar until its flow is suddenly interrupted by the Rock. Forced upwards, its moisture condenses and the

49

solitary cloud forms. No doubt it was one of nature's many wonders, but we had all looked forward to the day when we could leave it behind and sail out into the sunshine.

The first day of July 2013 was that day. At 14.25 we slipped our moorings and headed out to sea, destined for Gran Canaria via Madeira. Our timing was fortuitous as, unbeknown to us, clouds of a different nature were gathering above Gibraltar. They were political storm clouds as once again the governments of Spain and Great Britain engaged in yet another war of threats and gestures that have long characterised their uneasy relationship over this tiny but desirable rocky promontory.

The trigger was an argument over fishing rights and was exacerbated by Gibraltar dropping huge concrete blocks into the disputed waters to create an artificial reef. One side claimed it was to protect marine-life and the other side counter-claimed that it was to wreck fishing nets. In a mature response, Spanish divers were dispatched to erect the red and yellow flag of Spain on the submerged concrete blocks to declare their sovereignty over them. And so it went on, with the ordinary people on both sides having to live under a new cloud, not of their making.

More pertinent to us, there was yet another cloud phenomenon that we did not know about, this one awaiting us in Gran Canaria. It is known as the panza de burro, or 'donkey's belly', and is a cloud formation caused by trade winds laden with moisture becoming trapped between the hills of the various islands that make up the Canaries. The good news is that this cloud only affects the northern-most tip of Gran Canaria, producing overcast skies while the rest of the island is bathed in sunshine. The bad news is that the

Peurto de Las Palmas marina to which we were headed is at the northern-most tip of Gran Canaria! In the words of Victor Meldrew, "I don't believe it!"

There was, however, a lot of sailing to be done to take us from the cloud of Gibraltar to the cloud of Peurto de Las Palmas, and what wonderful sailing it turned out to be. We motored out of the marina, Europe on our starboard side and Africa on our port. Minutes later, Europe was on our port side and Africa on starboard as we circled back, boathook in hand, to retrieve one of our fenders that had been accidently dropped overboard. Despite that false start, we were soon headed the right way again, a friendly wind behind us and our genoa sail poled out to capture it.

To our delight, a pod of dolphins joined us, playing in our bow wave for a few minutes before leaving us to it. Flying fish then came to have a look at us; a spectacle we had never seen before. Soon after that, it was the turn of the seabirds to entertain us, reeling and wheeling above us and then swooping down and skimming the sea surface in precise correlation with the movement of the waves, seemingly without the slightest flicker of their wings. None of us was a twitcher, but our on-board bird book indicated that these enthralling seabirds belonged to the extensive family of Shearwaters. Whatever they were, their awesome, effortless skills were a joy to behold.

After about three hours, the Rock of Gibraltar had faded into the distance, the wind was comfortably on our beam and our speed under sail was a very respectable 5 to 6 knots. Eventually, even the mountains of Morocco disappeared from sight; only sea could then be seen on every side. That was an odd feeling, first experienced I believe by a man named

Noah who was the very first ARC participant, although he spelled it ARK.

The first night at sea

"I must go down to the seas again, to the lonely sea and the sky,
I left my vest and pants there, I wonder if they're dry."

This little rhyme made me giggle when I was a schoolboy, and still makes me smile today. It was years later before I realised that it — or something very like it - was attributed to Spike Milligan, and that he had based it on John Masefield's well known poem, 'Sea Fever'. As we sailed beyond the last trace of light and into the black of night, the real words of Sea Fever came back to me.

"I must go down to the seas again, to the lonely sea and the sky,
and all I ask is a tall ship and a star to guide her by."

I knew Second Wind was not a tall ship in the true sense of the words, but it was quite tall, and Chris showed me that helming at night was so much easier when we let ourselves be guided by conveniently located stars rather than trying to watch the compass and steer at the same time. He further cautioned me that, because of the earth's rotation, most stars seemingly move five degrees westward every twenty minutes, requiring us periodically to fix our focus on a different star. We still took sneaky glances at the compass for reassurance, but it was good to realise that, should all else fail, the stars remain a reliable navigational aid. In bygone days, many a ship has floundered on cloudy nights for want of 'a star to guide her by'.

It was our first night at sea and, once beyond the reach of all light pollution, was memorable and delightful. We had never seen a night sky like it. The heavens were a mass of stars; thousands of them, all clearly visible. And as we watched, almost transfixed, the stars would be unexpectedly joined by meteors, streaking through the stratosphere with the sudden brilliance of faraway fireworks. I shared my first night watch duty with Robin whose knowledge of stars and planets was helpful to me as, under his guidance, constellations took on shape and form in a way I had not seen before.

But nature had an even more enchanting surprise in store. I had expected to see thousands of lights twinkling in the night sky, but I had not expected to see thousands of similar lights glinting and glimmering in the sea as well. Yet as our bow cut through the water, that was what we saw, like countless glow-worms cascading through our bow wave, hurrying and scurrying every which way. It was mesmerising to watch. As if it was not enough for Robin to outshine me on his knowledge of stars, he also knew about this watery phenomenon too, calling it by its name - phosphorescence. I was captivated by it, and determined to find out more when I could next get my hands on Google.

That was a mistake. With its normal efficiency, Google later helped me to learn that the sea-lights we saw are emitted when luciferin, a flavin pigment, is oxidised in the presence of the enzyme luciferace. Who cares! Such a cold, forensic analysis belies the wonder of it. My thinking was in danger of becoming trapped like that of Thomas Gradgrind, the notorious headmaster penned by Charles Dickens in his Hard Times novel. Gradgrind's philosophy was, "Never wonder.

By means of addition, subtraction, multiplication and division, settle everything somehow, and never wonder." I disagree. It is absolutely right to wonder when something is wonderful. Having given William Wordsworth a hard time over his dubious knowledge of clouds, he redeems himself in his 'The Tables Turned' poem in which he urges us to "Let Nature be our teacher...she has a world of ready wealth our minds and hearts to bless." With educational books in mind, he continued:

"Enough of Science and of Art;
Close up those barren leaves,
Come forth, and bring with you a heart
That watches and receives."

I believe Wordsworth could have taught Gradgrind a thing or two. The wonder of phosphorescence is not in how it happens but in that it *does* happen, part of nature's 'ready wealth, our minds and hearts to bless', and there was blessing in it as we simply 'watched and received'. I could not imagine anyone witnessing this delight of nature without unalloyed joy in their hearts. Except, that is, the unfortunate captain and crew of the last German U-Boat to be sunk in the First World War. Apparently, so my research unearthed, his periscope left such a glowing wake that it gave away the boat's position and led to its destruction by Allied forces. How fearful it must have been to sail the seas at time of war, but for us, we enjoyed every moment. All too soon, the darkness started to give way to light and the remaining lines of John Masefield's first stanza took on fresh meaning:

"And the wheel's kick and the wind's song and the white sail's shaking.
And a grey mist on the sea's face, and a grey dawn breaking."

I guessed John Masefield had done some night-sailing of his own and saw, as we saw, the colour grey in a new light. As dawn broke, the sea and sky took on different shades of greyness, slowly distinguishing themselves from each other. As the light level continued to rise, lifting with it the also-grey morning mist, so the grey shades became increasingly differentiated. But do not be mistaken into thinking that those grey upon grey hues were in any way dull or depressing. Far from it. They provided a soft and soothing backdrop to a new day being ushered in, and somehow brought a refreshing restfulness to those of us seeing out the night watch, lifting our spirits and making us feel less tired than we ought from those hours of forced alertness. It may, of course, all look and feel very different in stormy conditions, but we were not to find that out until the rally itself.

Bad news aboard

One of our key pieces of equipment could not be tested until we were at sea and that was our new single side-band radio. I am not technical but, in a nutshell, it operates at a very low frequency but has an enormous range. The ARC guidelines encouraged every yacht to have one, as it enables crews to stay in contact with those at home when conventional communications were way out of range. Although Chris had installed the SSB radio in Gibraltar, we were unable to test it there as its low frequency could not compete against the plethora of electronic noise that invisibly fills the airwaves over such city-based marinas. Out to sea, however, it came into its own, and Chris was delighted to receive a reply to a test email he had initiated before we had set sail.

We had envisaged that the SSB email connection would have

kept us abreast of helpful news about wind and weather. As it turned out, the news we received was much more grave. Glyn's father had suddenly passed away. Glyn shouldered this saddest of news in stoic fashion and would continue to play a full role in our voyage until we reached Madeira, from where he would fly home to be with his family, taking our thoughts with him.

Food for thought

"The lovely thing about cruising is that planning usually turns out to be of little use." (Dom Degnon, author of Sails Full And By)

Our passage to Madeira took five days and five nights, the vast majority under sail. Second Wind performed faultlessly and we were able to test our planning in real conditions, especially our plans for keeping ourselves fed and watered. It would not be true to say, like Dom Degnon, that our planning turned out to be of little use, but there were some surprises.

The biggest surprise was how quickly our biscuits softened and our fresh produce wilted. Fruit and vegetables that we felt sure would have easily survived the relatively short trip, such as pears, carrots and peppers, quickly deteriorated in the heat. We rescued what we could by throwing together a new dish called 'curried everything' but some of our supplies proved beyond saving and so became a watery smorgasbord of fancy fish food. Apples and onions, however, proved their worth and easily stayed the course with us.

Another lesson learned on the food front was that our menu was a tad too fancy. Although we had laughed with Chris about entering the 'women's world' of cooking, we could cook. In fact, we probably deserved several Michelin stars for some of the dinners we prepared at sea, but in the cold light of day, the hot light of the galley took up too much of our time.

Ian's paella was admittedly the culinary triumph that it promised to be, but it did take him a good hour-and-a-half to prepare and cook, and then another hour or so to remove the black flecks from it. He had at first assumed that the black bits simply occurred naturally in the cooking process, but later realised that they were in fact shreds of Teflon that once coated the wok he was using, but now coated the cashews. He did confess to the presence of Teflon flecks before we ate. "It should slip down fine then", quipped Robin, and it did slip down very fine indeed. We survived. The wok did not. Ian had also maintained that only fresh basil would do for his recipe. I cannot prove it, but my guess was that we were the only yacht sailing the seas that day with its own live herb garden in a pot fixed to the saloon wall by bungee cords.

Even after the paella had been enjoyed, we dutifully continued to water the herb pot throughout our voyage in case another recipe called for it, such as Glyn's wonderful Moroccan vegetable stew with harissa paste. Once again, a masterpiece of a meal but, with hindsight, similarly expensive in terms of time and gas, not to mention the hour it took us to find the harissa in the first place, when we had been back in Gibraltar. Of course, any one of our wives would have told us that the supermarket staff could easily have directed us straight to the paste in a jiffy, had we but asked; but asking directions is something a chap simply does not do. Back on board, we reverted to various combinations of pasta, fresh vegetables and tinned mince, all stirred together in a single pot. Easy to prepare, easy on the palate, and easy on our resources. And although we did not, we could have dispensed with the herb garden.

It had only been a couple of days into our voyage before our gratitude surfaced to that experienced ocean-sailor who persuaded us in Gibraltar to prepare some meals in advance. That was because our culinary skills, however well honed, took a bashing when sea-sickness struck. Who and why sea-sickness hits is a lottery, but hit it does. On our voyage, my brother and I were fortunate to avoid the marine malady, but Robin and Ian both succumbed for a day or two, and Glyn was nauseated too. The trio found it more comfortable being on deck with their heads in buckets rather than below deck with their heads in cook books – another reason behind our decision to jettison the cordon bleu approach to cooking.

Although Robin, Glyn and Ian had felt more than lousy as they endured their bucket time, all three were encouraged by how well they felt once the nausea had passed and their sea legs had kicked in. If there is a best thing about sea-sickness, it is its temporary nature.

Throughout the voyage, we kept a tally of how much fresh water we used and measured that against our quota of two litres per person, per day. We also experimented with differently flavoured bread mixes, baking a loaf each day for our lunches. Friendly competition emerged between us as to who could bake the best-looking bread and which was the favoured flavour. Glyn won, although he did have more attempts than the rest of us put together. By a country mile, the favourite bread mix flavour was Parmesan and Sun Dried Tomato, which not only filled the boat with a wonderful aroma during its cooking, but also gave a convincing imitation of the taste of pizza, when we came to eat it.

We were also amazed how much long-life milk had improved since our childhood memories of that dreadful UHT stuff. The brand we bought was easily good enough to use on our cereals and, in fact, was hard to distinguish from fresh milk. After a while we had soon settled into a satisfying routine of cereal and fruit for breakfast, sandwiches for lunch and a full 'one-pot' meal in the evening, plus fruit, nuts and biscuits to nibble on between meals.

New lessons learned

Through the nights, we paired up and operated a four hours on, four hours off watch system, the two on watch swapping over the helm duty every half-hour. It worked well, although a couple of important lessons emerged. First, making up cuppa-soups proved a simple and nourishing way to sustain ourselves through the night watches. The lesson learned, however, was to always ensure that the cups were in the confined safety of the galley sink during the making of the soups. On one occasion, while he returned the kettle to the stove, Robin had left the made-up soups on the galley worktop. He then spent an hour on his hands and knees mopping up a messy mixture of mulligatawny and mushroom soups, which had flown off the surface as Second Wind did battle with a particularly big wave.

The second lesson we learned was to never ask Chris what to wear at sea. We had done, at one of our planning meetings. With that same air of authority displayed by Michael Fish in October 1987, reassuring the nation that no damaging winds were coming our way, Chris confidently asserted that we could expect nothing but warm weather day and night and, in his words, "Only T-shirts and shorts are required." In reality, although the days were warm, our night watches were spent snuggled into our foul-weather jackets with their fleece-lined collars pulled right up to our ears to defend against the chill. This is not something Chris is likely to forget as the rest of us will ensure he never does.

Being in full foul-weather gear was not a problem until nature called. And being over 50, she called us quite often! On the yacht, there was an art to taking a tinkle when encased in cumbersome clothing, especially in heavy swells. In short, we needed more hands than we had been born with. At home, simply standing astride a lavatory pan is all a chap has to do, with gravity doing the rest. At sea, with the yacht heeled over, we had to be more calculating as to where we stood for gravity to hit the target. Rather than adopting a 'hit and miss' approach, the most successful stance proved to be standing widely astride with our heels hard up against the wall opposite the WC pan. We then leaned forward until our forehead rested against the facing wall, the pan in our eyeline below us. Just like the successful milking stool design before it, this provided a three-point-of-contact stance that was surprisingly stable and, importantly, left both hands free for other things.

Adopting this stance reminded me of a time I once used the lavatory at a friend's house. When seated on his loo, I noticed a tantalisingly small sign placed just above the skirting board in front of me. Leaning forward to read it, the tiny writing said, 'You are now operating at an angle of forty-five degrees'. For him, it was a joke. For us, it was indeed the most stable stand-up angle of operation, and saved much mopping.

On the whole, all of our planning had proved more good than bad, building our confidence for what lay ahead. By the afternoon of Saturday 6th July, Madeira was in our sights. On seeing land, Ian had set for ourselves a new target of getting to the marina in time to see the British and Irish Lions take on Australia in the deciding match of the Rugby Union Lions tour.

Unfortunately, by the time we had Second Wind safely secured on a pontoon, we arrived at the marina's TV lounge only a couple of minutes before the final whistle was blown. That was a little disappointing, as we missed seeing all the points scored as the Lions thumped Australia 41 to 16. However, we were still in good time to score a point of our own by chirping, "Have a nice day" to three burly Australians as they despondently left the lounge. They did not reply. Perhaps they did not hear us. Shame.

The final leg

After saying a sad farewell to Glyn, we stayed in Madeira's Quinta Do Lorde marina just one night. The following day at 13.30, when Andy Murray was no doubt psyching himself up for his epic Wimbledon showdown with Novak Djokovic, we were psyching ourselves up for the final 300 nautical miles of our journey. We missed Glyn of course, but how good it was to have Ian to make up the four, not least because it enabled us to continue experimenting with the watch system we had planned for the ARC rally, and because it gave us an extra pair of hands to tend the herb garden!

As we sailed, we wanted at some time to test flying the light wind cruising chute that we carried on board. Thankfully, there was a period in our journey when the wind dropped enough for us to fly the chute, but unfortunately, that particular light wind was too intermittent; it was sufficient to fill the sail but not constant enough to keep it filled.

More worryingly, we also noticed that the lines of the cruising chute were snagging on our bow navigation lights, threatening to snap them off. To avoid this happening, we quickly collapsed the sail and aborted our test, knowing that some sort of bowsprit would need to be fabricated to keep the lines away from the light fittings. That sort of fabrication is meat and drink to Chris, but would have to wait until we were home. Second Wind has many things but not a carpentry workshop on board. Still, the test was very worthwhile; far better to have ironed out any snags before the rally rather than to discover them during the event.

The four of us quickly got into a sailing routine that seemed to work, and we continued to enjoy each other's company. We had each brought books, believing there would be long periods of time with nothing to do, but found that we enjoyed just talking and watching much more than reading. Being blokes together, we discussed some very deep issues such as the comparative length of time it took our self-close loo seats at home to descend, or whether toilet paper should hang from the front of the roll or behind it. Or, when making instant coffee, whether the milk should be added before or after the hot water? There was no meeting of minds on that important coffee debate (although the right answer is 'before').

Small pods of dolphins continued to visit us from time to time, mostly during the night, staying and playing for just a few minutes each time. A variety of sea birds entertained us during the day, amazing us not only with their awesome acrobatics but also with how far they could fly from the shore to find their food and to keep us amused. And the beauty and clarity of the night sky, coupled with those intriguing phosphorescent sea-lights, continued to delight us.

Our biggest surprise was seemingly having the sea to ourselves. It was back in 1801 when Horatio Nelson had been confronted by many Danish ships in the Battle of Copenhagen, but pretended that they were not there, holding a telescope to his blind eye and supposedly uttering those famous words, "I see no ships." Whether or not he said those precise words, as opinions differ, we did not need to pretend. There were virtually no ships to see. Once away from the sight of land, we saw only three or four other vessels during the entire voyage, and only a couple of those close up.

One of them could have been very close up indeed, had not one of us steered away. Amazingly, despite people saying that big tankers do not give way to sail boats whatever the rules of the sea might say, the tanker that was heading our way did indeed alter its course to avoid us. Well done Captain! With its stern disappearing into the distance and with our faith in human nature restored, we decided to throw out a sea anchor and treat ourselves to a swim.

"The goal is not to sail the boat but rather to help the boat sail herself." (John Rousmaniere, author of many nautical books.)

By Tuesday, July 9th we were fast approaching the end of our time at sea. In one way I was sorry. I had enjoyed learning sailing skills from the others and putting them into practice, especially when at the wheel. My tendency, as a novice, was to fight the helm in order to keep strictly to a compass bearing, making big movements on the wheel, first one way and then the other, constantly correcting over-corrections. After a while, this was exhausting and, worse, slowed the boat down as the rudder blade was too often pushing the water side-on rather than slicing through it. This relatively long voyage helped us all, but me particularly, to get a better feel for helming and, occasionally, even mastering the boat in the manner John Rousmaniere describes, with sails set just right for the conditions and Second Wind keeping to course all by herself, with only the lightest of touches from us. What a joy!

Land ahoy!

We knew we were nearing the end of our journey, but we still could not see land by the time the evening light was fading. Strangely, although we had utter confidence in the satellite navigation equipment, assuring us that land was just over the horizon, until we could see it for ourselves, a bit of us remained unconvinced. We all strained our eyes scanning that horizon.

Eventually, something that started as nothing more than a faint glow in the far distance, slowly took shape and form. The top tip of Gran Canaria was revealing itself. We had waited a long time for this moment and now enjoyed it, although we knew it would still be hours yet before we reached the harbour entrance. We also knew how tricky it would be to navigate ourselves into a place we had never seen or been before, especially in the dead and dark of night. Fortunately for the rest of us, that responsibility would fall to Chris.

A little after midnight, with the coastline lights of Gran Canaria becoming ever more distinct, the radio crackled into life. It was a coastguard message to all shipping. Red distress flares had been sighted south of Tenerife and any nearby craft were urged to keep a lookout. The message was repeated every ten minutes or so. We were too far distant to be of help but it still subdued our mood. It was not a nice feeling to know that fellow sailors who, like us, must have thought themselves safe and secure in their vessel, might now possibly be in mortal danger with no help to hand. We had enjoyed having the sea to ourselves and not seeing another boat for days at a time, but how frightening that solitude must be in different circumstances.

A couple more hours passed before we saw clearly the flashing green light that indicated the port entrance. We furled our sails and fired up the engine. The next hour was probably the most tense of the whole voyage. Peurto de Las Palmas is huge and alive with activity even at night, with many ships coming and going, or just lying at anchor but giving the impression of coming or going; the lights of stationary boats set against the backdrop of lights ashore can be very confusing. All of us were wide awake, either on deck scanning the shoreline or below deck, checking the chart plotter or referring to the almanac that described the entrance configuration of the marina part of the port.

At last we saw the marina entrance lights and headed for them. We were nearly there. In readiness, we tied the fenders along the port side of the yacht and set them at a level which we hoped would be right for the height of the marina's pontoons, but our hands were poised to change them quickly if we had guessed wrong. We had guessed right, and Second Wind was soon tied alongside the visitors' pontoon. We took to our beds for what was left of the night. We had done it!

Back in Gibraltar, we had all wondered, openly and secretly, what it would be like to be at sea for so long and how we would cope. Well, we had coped. Coped very well, in fact. And not just coped but enjoyed coping. Even if the voyage had been longer, we knew we would have coped with that too. That encouraged us as we thought forward to our Atlantic crossing, which would be more than three times the distance we had just travelled, in seas less hospitable and in winds a good deal stronger.

Adventures in the washrooms

Coincidentally, about a decade ago, I had spent a week's holiday crewing on a yacht sailing around the island of Gran Canaria, mooring each night at different marinas, including once at Las Palmas. My abiding memory from that holiday was how hard Gran Canarian marinas worked to ensure that trips to their washrooms were an adventure in themselves. As we had approached the marina these years later, I had wondered whether things had changed. They had not. Let me explain.

During the morning of our arrival, after the marina office had opened and we had booked in, we moved Second Wind from the visitors' berth to the pontoon that was to be her new home until the ARC start in November. One of the marina's washroom facilities was just across the marina service road from our pontoon, which was good news. It was handy to have a convenience nearby. Using the heads on board Second Wind had to be limited, because the holding tanks could not be emptied within the confines of the marina.

The nearby washroom had two WC cubicles. In common with my earlier recollections, neither of the cubicles had a lock and the doors were hung such that they tended to swing open rather than closed. The lavatory pans were sited just awkwardly enough to make it nigh impossible to hold the door shut from a seated position either with hand or foot.

On closer inspection, only one of the cubicles had paper in the dispenser, enticing me to choose that one. But because my attention had been cleverly distracted by the availability of paper, I had simply assumed that the lavatory seat was fixed to the sanitary ware. It was not. All was well until it came to that time to lean sideways, paper in hand. One leg, do not forget, was already in the air, trying to hold the door shut. On lifting the other leg, my weight distribution changed sufficiently for the seat to shoot from under me, depositing the majority of my rear end in the pan. I eventually left the cubicle relieved in every sense of the word; relieved physically, relieved emotionally, and relieved specifically that I had managed to keep my trousers dry despite both legs having flayed about in some disorder.

With my guard down, I had ventured to the nearby basin to wash my hands. The single tap on the basin was the self-closing type, whereby a downward push on the top would normally release a trickle of water for a specified period of seconds. But this one was set mischievously to dispense water with great ferocity and velocity. Having pressed the top, a deluge slammed into the basin. The curvature of the bowl was seemingly designed to divert that powerful torrent directly onto the front of my hitherto dry trousers!

You may think all of that was coincidental rather than conspiratorial. Really? Then let me describe the showers in the same washroom. It was true that the shower doors did not suffer the same shortcomings as the doors to the WC cubicles, but that was only because there were no doors! There was half a wall protruding from one side of each cubicle. That gave half my body some privacy. Mounted on the far wall were two taps, both again of the self-closing type. They were set far enough from each other to make it impossible to operate both with the same hand at the same time, although one hand was all I had available as the other had to hold the soap and shampoo, there being no shelf. My only alternative was to place those items on the floor and squat down to reach for them as and when needed.

The hot tap, unless continuously depressed, spouted water for only one-and-a-half seconds. Cunningly, the water temperature was set so hot that it had to be tempered with cold water. The cold water tap, once depressed, gave about eight seconds of flow. So picture it. One of my hands had to permanently hover over the hot tap plunger while the other hand needed to work at the speed of light, reaching down to pick up and dispense soap and shampoo, applying it and lathering it, but diverting every seven seconds or so to keep adding cold water to the hot. I emerged clean but exhausted. The only plus I could see to negotiating marina washrooms in Gran Canaria was that it made using the heads on a yacht a doddle, even in the stormiest of seas.

A last evening treat

After arriving at the marina, we had a few days in hand to enjoy the surrounding city before our flights home. Las Palmas was well worth exploring, especially the old part, steeped in history and nautical heritage. Having immersed ourselves in the past, we then had to bring ourselves back to the present, which was comparatively mundane but nonetheless important. We located the nearest supermarket which we would need to visit when we returned in November, to buy the remainder of the provisions needed for the ARC rally, and to purchase the ingredients required to pre-prepare a few dinners to see us through the sea-sickness period.

Robin and Ian flew home the day before Chris and me, and the two of us decided that, for our last evening together, we would eat at a particularly enticing fish restaurant in the marina complex. We had walked past its outside tables on numerous occasions, salivating at the food we saw on the plates of eaters. On that last day, it was our turn to sample its seafood, which did not disappoint and proved to be every bit as good as it looked. How could Glyn not like fish, we wondered?

At the table next to ours sat two retired ex-pats. We chatted with them at some length about the upcoming ARC adventure. They responded like so many others – "We wouldn't do that if you paid us!" We tried to assure them that the rally was by far the safest way to sail the Atlantic, although the restaurant was not helping our argument. For some reason best known to themselves, for the entire evening they projected onto the wall a film of the ill-fated 1998 Sydney to Hobart yacht race disaster.

For those who do not recollect that tragedy, the fleet of 115 yachts was ravaged by raging seas whipped up by 70 knot winds. The storm caused 5 yachts to sink and a further 66 retired damaged, some severely. A total of 55 crewmen had to be airlifted to safety. Tragically, 6 sailors perished. Although that was not the image we wanted to take home with us, we knew that the Sydney to Hobart disaster helped a great deal to improve safety equipment and procedures for future sailing races and rallies, including the ARC. It was sobering but true that, come November, we would be significantly safer because of that fateful day some 15 years earlier. The following day, we returned to England, happily with no suitcase drama to endure at Gatwick Airport.

Other yachts converge on Gran Canaria

We may have been back at home for a while, but our thoughts remained on the rally. We were relieved that Second Wind was safely secured at Gran Canaria, but we continued to think about the many other crews out there somewhere, following in our wake and sailing their yachts from wherever they were to the Las Palmas marina. Like us before them, they hoped they would arrive in good shape and in good time for the ARC start. Many faced journeys of over a thousand miles, a challenge for them as it had been for us. We wished them well and looked forward to meeting them.

However, the camaraderie generated by the ARC starts long before skippers and crews physically meet and greet one another in Gran Canaria. Firstly, with so many yachts making their way to the Canaries from similar starting points, it was inevitable that some would find themselves berthed in the same marinas en route, those chance encounters spawning early mateyness amongst competitors.

Perhaps because we had made our passage to Las Palmas rather earlier than most, we had not met any ARC boats on the way. Nonetheless, in the week or two before our flight back out to Gran Canaria to rejoin Second Wind, we entered into the spirit of things by starting to follow the blogs, or logs as the ARC calls them, being written by a number of the crews on their sea-journeys to the ARC start line.

Their logs were posted on the World Cruising Club website and, although many, they tended to follow a familiar format. Three topics dominated. The weather was one, and especially its impact on sea states, sailing speeds and sailor-sickness. The yacht was another, majoring particularly on the bits of it that unexpectedly failed to work, jammed fast, came apart or fell off. And the third was food and drink, with many bloggers describing their delicious dinners and deserts in mouth-watering detail.

Potentially dispiriting logs

There were, however, a couple of additional recurring themes in those logs that did not make the best of reading for us. One was the fact that some yachts were clearly achieving greater speeds than we had managed in similar wind conditions. This may not be as concerning as could first appear; they may simply be bigger boats. Of the 164 yachts entered into the ARC Cruising Division, 123 of them were longer than Second Wind's 42 foot length. All other things being equal, longer yachts would be faster than shorter ones.

This is all to do with waves. As if the ocean does not generate enough waves of its own, each boat creates another wave as its hull pushes up the water in front of it. The crest of this new wave is a little ahead of the boat's bow and it crests again under the boat's stern. It is the length of the trough between these two wave-crests that determines the maximum theoretical hull speed of a boat. This is beginning to sound a bit scientific, meaning snoringly boring, so I will stop there. The formula is not important. Suffice to say that the theoretical maximum hull speed through the water for our yacht is 8.5 knots, whereas it is 9.5 knots for a boat just ten feet longer. And one of the yachts we would be up against was a massive 72 footer with a theoretical hull speed of 12 knots! Yachts can travel faster than their theoretical hull speeds but it takes comparatively more power to do so.

On the surface, this may not appear fair for a race or rally, but those idiosyncrasies would be largely ironed out by the ARC handicap system that was designed to take account of the differing lengths and weights of the yachts. We were hoping that the handicap factor would work in our favour, lifting our eventual rally placing significantly higher than our actual finishing position; we needed all the help we could get!

The other thing that was slightly dispiriting to read was various crews describing how well their cruising chutes had performed in light winds, enabling good speeds to be maintained even after the wind had dropped. That was not music to our ears, given our failure to fly our chute successfully when we had experimented with it. If we could not fix that problem before the rally, and if the Atlantic winds turned out to be lighter than expected, not having the cruising chute available would put us at a serious disadvantage to other boats, and no handicap system would come to our rescue on that one.

To put our slight anxiousness into some kind of perspective, if we averaged a speed of 4.5 knots rather than 5 knots, over the 2,800 nautical miles to Saint Lucia, that 0.5 knot difference would add two full days and nights of sailing to our passage. So you see that, over long distances, squeezing just a fraction of a knot more speed out of the boat would be hugely significant. The cruising chute, if only we could fly it successfully, should be able to add at least a knot or two to our speed, in the right conditions.

Despite those one or two minor concerns, the many logs helped above all to convey the great enthusiasm there was for the ARC, with an unmistakable air of excitement rippling through them. It was clear that, for some, it was a dream come true, or an adventure of a lifetime. One crew commented that they were still pinching themselves at their good fortune of being involved. So were we. And Robin was further chuffed when Glyn reported that the crew of the boat NDS Darwin had blogged about their fishing success; just two days out from Las Palmas, they had landed a 90 pound yellowfin tuna. We would all be willing on Robin to catch a similar-sized supper for us although, should it happen, Glyn's cheers would probably be slightly hollow and he would not be first to reach for the frying pan and apron.

November 10th the second time around

Time moved on and it was now exactly a year to the day from when Chris had invited me to join Robin, Glyn and himself in this Atlantic adventure. The following day we would be flying from Gatwick back to Gran Canaria for the start of the rally. But that was a day away, and we had to pack before that.

Packing a suitcase for a week away is hard enough, but packing for at least six weeks away was a challenge in itself, especially when three or four of those weeks would be at sea, without access to shops or launderettes. Airlines too do not help, imposing the same 20 kilogram weight limit on our main baggage irrespective of our time away. Fortunately we had been able to leave our heavyweight all-weather clothing and a few other bits and pieces on the yacht from our previous sail, but it was still questionable whether my holdall would indeed hold all.

There was little we could do to reduce baggage volume and weight, apart from leaving some essentials at home and replacing them in Gran Canaria. Being all blokes, we did knock-about a few radical ideas in our planning meetings, particularly concerning underpants. We reasoned, for example, that we could wear them the right way round, then the wrong way round, then turn them inside-out and again wear them one way and then the other, rather than changing them altogether. This led us to ponder whether we could push that idea even further and only take two pairs of underpants with us; one to wear the entire time until we spotted Saint Lucia, and then, as that pair disintegrated into dust, donning a clean pair for our arrival and flight home. In the end, we decided simply to take all the shirts, socks and pants that we owned and accept that, at some point, we would have to endure wearing clothes that had been washed in sea water.

To make matters worse, over and above the everyday clothes we needed to pack, there were a few extra things to take, such as our favourite cuppa-soups and biscuits that were not available in Gran Canaria, a wig for the wig party and a fancy dress costume for another of the events organised by the ARC team. But even more than this, Chris had indeed designed a bowsprit for our cruising chute, and fabricated it out of solid oak that was more than a hundred years old, having originally been part of a church harmonium. That too had to fit somehow into our holdalls and, clever as he is, Chris has not yet designed one of those bottomless carpet bags as carried by Mary Poppins, which would have been ideal for the task.

Do not get me wrong, our new bowsprit was nothing like those enormous poles of old that used to protrude from the prow of ships, and were otherwise known as 'widowmakers', reflecting the danger of working on them. No, ours was only about three feet in length, but it still presented a challenge to pack without offending easyJet.

The lack of packing space meant that our fancy dress costumes had to be minimalist to be squeezed in. And they were. This was how it happened. We knew in advance that the party theme was to be 'fantasy world' but we were reticent about simply ordering any old costume from a store. Anyone could have done that. We wanted to apply some ingenuity and come up with something more thoughtful, but not bulky. However, as we discussed possibilities at one of our planning get-togethers, it soon became pretty obvious that none of us knew anything about the world of fantasy. We chuckled that the greatest example of 'fantasy world' would be for us to win the ARC rally.

But wait? Had we inadvertently struck on a good idea? We promptly found a supplier who would print our idea on four T-shirts. Separately, the words we asked to be printed were meaningless, but when we stood shoulder to shoulder, all wearing the T-shirts, the printed message across our four combined chests would read: 2013 ARC RALLY WINNERS, and below that, 'Fantasy World in the Extreme'. To round off the whole ensemble, we bought four cheap sets of sailor hats and collars. At the very least, all this would be easy to pack and should make for a good photo. It may even get a mention on the night!

However good our costumes were, we knew that, in all probability, we would not look very much like sailors on that party night. What was harder for me to accept was that I must not look very much like a sailor on any night. This came home to me when I had returned to the printers to pick up our newly-printed T-shirts. The proprietor took an interest and wanted to know what the ARC was all about. I told him of the Atlantic adventure, but as nonchalantly as I could, trying to make it sound like just another day at the office. I was brought down to earth with a bump when he responded, "That sounds great! And where do you fit in? Are you going to wave them off?" I left with the shirts, but humbled.

Chapter Four

The end of the beginning

November 11th – a day to remember

November 11th; Remembrance Day. What more appropriate day to recall those famous words of wartime Prime Minister, Winston Churchill, spoken 71 years ago almost to the day:

"Now this is not the end. It is not even the beginning of the end. But it is, perhaps, the end of the beginning." (Sir Winston Churchill, 10th November 1942)

It was after 'The Battle of Egypt' that Churchill spoke those stirring words. Chris and I find them moving because our dear dad had fought in that tide-turning battle, having been one of Field Marshall Montgomery's renowned desert rats. But Churchill's words also describe so well where we had got to in our adventure. Together with Glyn and Robin, so much had been achieved in terms of planning and preparing, training and travelling, yet not one inch of the rally had yet been sailed. Everything we had done over the preceding year still represented just the beginning. But November 11th 2013 was for us, at last, truly the end of the beginning.

Las Palmas transformed

At the crack of dawn we arrived at Gatwick Airport. In the departures area, we were relieved that we had no problems with checking-in our luggage, despite our holdalls carrying the oak bowsprit that happened to be the same size and shape as a sawn-off shotgun, numerous packets of bread mixes that had the same look and feel as heroin, and an electrical device that my brother had constructed for the galley which in essence was a plastic box with switches and lights on it and wire coiled around it. I had never seen a bomb, but if I imagined one, it would have looked the same.

The flight to Gran Canaria was uneventful and as we approached the island, the 'donkey's belly' was clearly visible from the aeroplane window, hanging over the port and marina of Las Palmas like clouds do. In that respect, nothing had changed. On reaching the marina, however, everything else had changed dramatically.

Back in September, we had left a quiet and peaceful place, full of mostly-empty yachts swaying gently on their moorings, the shops and restaurants open but not busy, and the adjacent bay attracting the odd yacht or two each day, dropping anchor to allow those on board to swim in the warm waters. In short, a pleasant but tranquil marine scene. But now an atmosphere of excitement had descended; there was a buzz in the air; one could sense that something big was happening.

The previously-empty bay was filled with yachts at anchor. They were the yachts that would normally be moored in the marina but had to vacate their berths to make room for the ARC yachts. Some of the rally boats were still on their way but the majority had already arrived. The ARC yachts were easy to spot because they were festooned with fluttering flags, the most prominent being the large blue 2013 ARC Rally flag. A few of them were also displaying ARC flags from previous years, showing that this was not their first attempt at the Atlantic crossing.

In addition, at the request of the organisers, the ARC yachts were dressed. This required each yacht to 'wear' its whole set of signal flags, running them from the bow, up to the top of the mast and down to the stern. Organising the string of signals was more involved than you might imagine. They had to be connected together, one by one. Each flag represents a different letter of the alphabet and some also convey a common message on their own, or coupled with one or two others, so there is an order in which they have to be connected, depending on what message is being conveyed. So as not to inadvertently convey a rude or indecent message, which is possible if all the flags and pennants are joined up haphazardly, there is a set sequence carefully prescribed by the Admiralty for the way a boat is dressed. The Admiralty's care extends not only to prevent potentially offensive messages in English but also in other languages too.

I have to say that, to me, they were just flags, and when they were all strung together, they became pretty bunting. I could not imagine the threat was high of a random Outer Mongolian with a detailed knowledge of marine signals passing by and happening to notice that a certain set of flags wished him a plague on all his houses. It seemed to me that a major amount of effort had been taken to avoid the tiniest of risks, but that is diplomacy for you, and we would be happy to comply when we got around to decorating our yacht. The last thing we wanted was for Second Wind to be inappropriately dressed.

Apart from hundreds of flags, there were hundreds of people too. They were everywhere; on the yachts, in the shops and filling the bars and restaurants. The pontoons were hives of activity as crews congregated for chats or worked on their boats, local shop staff delivered food and water, street vendors plied their trade and would-be travellers offered their services in the hope of finding a berth on one of the ARC yachts to take them to the Caribbean.

That said, successfully finding a berth might not have necessarily been the end of their troubles. In Chapter Two, I referred to the plight of the Robertson family. What I failed to mention was that a hitch-hiker of the sea had been given a space with the family on their ill-fated voyage. He must have been over the moon to have secured a ride in their 43 foot schooner for an around-the-world adventure of a lifetime. He was probably not so happy ending up with them in their tiny dinghy for 37 long days adrift, rubbing excruciating sea sores and nursing particularly tender buttocks.

But that was back in 1971; now there was no shortage of willing volunteers to share our travels with us. It was sad to turn away so many eager, polite and apparently qualified people who may well have been an asset to any crew, although the man who wanted us to take him because, in his words, he "had just been chucked off another yacht" may want to reconsider his sales pitch!

On café tables, lattes and laptops fought for space, the latte poured out and the laptop pored over as online weather charts were studied intently. The main chandlers became so busy that it had to operate a numbering system to most efficiently deal with its queue of customers, and the sailmakers, riggers and the boatyard were all places of frenzied activity.

The various eateries remained open long into the night to meet demand, and I was pleased to see that the fish restaurant we visited last time was no longer projecting images of yachting doom and disaster, carrying as it did, the subliminal message, 'today you may be eating fishes but tomorrow the fishes may be eating you'. Instead, their wall-mounted screen displayed pictures of expensive yachts gliding effortlessly towards Caribbean sunsets, steered by bronzed Brazilians being admired by glamorous girls. That image was just as unrealistic as the disaster one, but was much more palatable.

And the biggest change of all? I could not believe it; in the marina washroom by our pontoon, the airborne loo seat had been properly secured to the lavatory pan and bolts had been fitted to the WC cubicle doors!

At the centre of all this activity was the ARC village – a group of portacabins housing the ARC team's offices, reception area, shop and meeting point. It was here that we were welcomed, registered our arrival, received our welcome pack containing a wealth of helpful information, and were presented with our Rally number – 193. It was not a random number but rather represented the likely finishing position of Second Wind, all other things being equal, based on our yacht's size and weight.

Yellow is the colour

Down through the ages, just mentioning the colour of a uniform was all that needed to be said to describe the character of those who wore it. The Black Watch in Scotland and the Black & Tans in Ireland all have their place in history. Likewise, green berets still speak of a commando's strength, or red berets of a paratrooper's bravery. Back in the 1930s and 40s, this colour-recognition was extended to holiday camps. Billy Butlin's famous Redcoats and Fred Pontin's

Bluecoats became known to thousands of holiday-makers as people determined to make their stay more pleasurable than it would otherwise have been. And without a doubt, the same could be said of the World Cruising Club's team of Yellow-Shirts.

The success of the 2013 ARC Rally would be in no small part down to that ARC team of people; about two dozen yellow-shirted helpers, many bilingual and all of them cheerful. Like the red and blue coats before them, they too succeeded in making our stay the best it could be. They hosted parties and dinners, organised events and seminars, took photographs of us and for us, facilitated contact and discounts with local shops and businesses, provided a shuttle-bus service in the marina, advised us on the weather, and more besides. In general, they made themselves available to answer our questions and point us in the right direction at the right time. And I am sure that, behind the scenes, they were doing many more things to ensure a safe and fun event for all of us. They were superb ambassadors for the Club, and greatly added to our rally experience.

The final fortnight

We had allowed ourselves a full fortnight to make our final preparations as well as giving ourselves time to enjoy some of the ARC pre-start activities. There were a few jobs that we knew we needed to do and, on unlocking Second Wind, a few more that we did not know about. A couple of small surprises awaited us. First, although we had cleared up the mushroom and mulligatawny mayhem from the soup-spill previously mentioned, we obviously had not done it thoroughly enough, as the yacht's lower mahogany surfaces were now displaying numerous areas of mould that coincided with where the soups had splashed. The other surprise was on opening the cutlery drawer and finding that every knife, fork and spoon was rusty; a consequence of washing them up in sea water on our previous voyage. Both of those 'surprise finds' would be quick and easy to rectify, and we added them to our short list of things to be done over the coming days.

As we unpacked our holdalls, there was another surprise, this one relating to the perception of others as to what we were doing. Back home, when I had first announced that I was going to try to sail the Atlantic Ocean, one of my brothers-in-law (another Chris) kindly bought me a camera, assuring me that it would work underwater. I thanked him but pointed out that I was not planning to be under the water but rather on top of it. This would hardly be worth mentioning except that Glyn produced from his luggage the exact same model of camera, bought for him by his work colleagues who had similarly assured him of its ability to work underwater. At this, Robin showed us a plastic cover given to him by one of his relatives to protect his iPhone underwater. We hoped we would not get as wet as some people obviously thought we would!

Our first day back in Gran Canaria passed without further incident. Having unpacked, we agreed between us who would sleep where. Glyn chose the fore cabin, sharing the triangular bed with a big bag containing our storm jib-sail. In theory, this front cabin should not be so lively during the rally as previously described because the wind was more likely to be behind us, causing a rolling movement rather than the more uncomfortable up-and-down motion of the bow. Having the jib-sail sack wedged beside him should also prevent Glyn from rolling too far one way or the other.

Robin decided that he was happy to use one of the coffin-like bunks. The fact that the bunks offered a tight fit would actually be an advantage if and when the weather turned stormy, which it would do, but more about that later. He chose the upper bunk for his bed, using the lower one for the stowage of his belongings.

That left the big double bed in the owners' cabin for me to share with my brother. We recalled that we had not shared a double bed since we were young boys. We remembered the night well. Our beloved black labrador, Sally, had died and we were heart-broken. In an attempt to cheer us, our mum and dad let us stay up later than usual so we could watch Perry Mason on the black & white TV, and then they let us sleep in their big bed. Here we were, more than 50 years later, back together in a double bed; except now, there was a stout canvas lee-cloth secured from the ceiling and running down the centre of the mattress, not only to protect us in wild weather but also providing a degree of privacy that we had not worried about when we were kids.

With our sleeping arrangements put to bed, so to speak, we spent the next hour or so stringing together our signal flags in the prescribed order, and hoisting them to dress Second Wind. Then, in the early evening, we attended our first ARC Sundowner event. The Sundowners were hosted by the yellow-shirts virtually every evening, running from 18.30 to 20.00. Apart from a great opportunity to meet other crews over complimentary drinks, each Sundowner was sponsored by an organisation or business offering goods or services that ARC participants could well find helpful. Sometimes, for example, it gave us the chance to sample local produce, whereas another evening would be sponsored, say, by a firm of shipping agents offering their services to those who, like

Chris, had decided to have their yachts shipped back from the Caribbean after the ARC rally was over.

The Sundowners were very relaxed and friendly events, and helpful too in meeting folk from the other boats. What diverse people we all were. A few were owners of luxurious yachts who had hired an experienced crew to sail their boat across the ocean and to serve them while doing it. Some were people who had paid for the privilege of crewing. There were people who made their living from sailing and others who sailed just for pleasure. Some had made the crossing a few times before but most, like us, had never sailed an ocean and had come together solely for the adventure.

It was a pleasure getting to know at least some of these people, striking up happy banter in the main, although my small-talk did let me down on one occasion. I found myself talking to a South African skipper and, having recognised from their accents that there were quite a few crew from that country, I remarked to him that sailing must be in the DNA of South Africans. He somewhat curtly reminded me that, historically, it was us British who ruled the waves and, unlike other nations, when we sailed to nice islands, we took them over and kept them!

I assured him that we had given most of them back, but knew he had a strong case. In fact, and I was glad he did not know this, back in 1595, there had been a skirmish known as the Battle of Las Palmas, when our Sir Francis Drake tried his best to gain the very island on which we were standing, but without success. Had Margaret Thatcher been Prime Minister in 1595, there might well have been a different outcome. Despite that one moment of awkwardness, the Sundowners were popular and well attended; another successful ARC-team initiative in their determined efforts to make our adventure memorable and as well supported as possible.

Not yet ready

The first three full days of our final fortnight were relatively busy for us. The old petrol-driven generator strapped to our deck was an essential piece of equipment but although we could start it, we could not keep it running for more than a few minutes. It needed a complete overhaul but that required the removal of nuts and screws that had rusted solid over many years and took an age to budge.

It was important for us to get the generator working. Without using the yacht's motor to charge the batteries, the only mechanisms we had for generating power at sea were a wind-powered generator and a couple of solar panels, both mounted on a tubular gantry on the stern of Second Wind and both, of course, weather dependent. Chris had calculated that they should be enough to power our navigational equipment and lights, but not the fridge as well. Ordinarily, a fridge could be deemed a luxury, but we really needed it for Glyn's diabetes medicines, which had to be kept cool. It took most of a day to prise open the generator and service it.

Another time-consuming job was sewing a suede cover around the wheel; it was a very big wheel in comparison with the very small stitches required, but Robin painstakingly stitched the cover all the way round while I did my best to hold it in place. This too took some hours, although it must be said that Robin became increasingly impressive with the needle and thread. If the bottom ever falls out of the auction business, he could easily turn his hand to being whatever the male equivalent of a seamstress is called.

The reason for applying this suede covering was to protect our hands, should the tropical sun heat up the metal wheel to an uncomfortable temperature. Many of the boats, especially the more modern ones, had automated steering powered by inboard diesel generators, but we did not have the power available to drive our auto-pilot system, so our hands would need to be on the wheel virtually every hour of the day and night. As it turned out, all four of us were to end the rally with blistered fingers from working the wheel for so long.

Incidentally, the strip of suede was only about three inches wide and not more than ten feet long; had it been bought at a haberdashery it would have cost about £7.50 but as it was for a boat, it retailed at a staggering £75! Perhaps the word 'nautical' derives from the fact that retailers could add a 'naut' to the price of anything to do with sailing!

Other tasks that occupied our time included Chris fitting the new oak bowsprit to anchor our light-wind cruising chute, Robin preparing his fishing tackle, and Glyn and I negotiating the local supermarket for the remainder of the non-perishable provisions needed. Again, the ARC set-up made shopping much more straightforward than it otherwise would have been. Within the ARC village, the HyperDino supermarket chain had a representative on hand to direct us, provide us with discount vouchers, and even interpret for us so we could discern the difference between tins of whole tomatoes, chopped tomatoes, puréed tomatoes and tomato paste! He too was a credit to his employer. Once the shopping was done, everything was packed by the store into large crates that were then delivered to our boat within an hour. It was an impressive service by any standard.

Included on our shopping list was bottled water. As we had no watermaker, we would have to carry all the fresh water we might possibly need, and then some more just in case. All told, we ended up carrying some 650 litres of fresh water weighing in at about two-thirds of a ton, more than twice the weight of the four of us put together! No wonder those racers do not carry more than they have to. We had our two litres per person per day quota in plastic bottles; we had supplementary water in the freshwater tank; we had emergency water in the Grab Bag and life-raft; we had extra water in containers in the deck lockers, and we had contingency water under the floor-boards! We were in just as much danger of drowning on board as overboard.

What a difference a day makes

Thursday, 14th November can best be described as a day of ups and downs. That was true for our emotions as well as our signal flags. The day started well. We had gathered together and laid out all of our safety equipment in readiness for the obligatory ARC safety inspection. Placed all together, it covered the table and the seats in the saloon and made one realise just how much had to be carried in case of the worst happening. The inspection covered our radios, the contents of our emergency Grab Bag, our life-raft, the three different types of distress flares we carried, the first aid kit, our life-jackets and harnesses, our man-overboard equipment, the two sea anchors, our emergency steering bar, and so on.

Just in terms of hailing help in a distress situation, the extent and diversity of what we carried was mind-boggling. At one end of the scale was the simple whistle that could be heard only by those in earshot. At the high-tech end was our EPIRB (Emergency Position-Indicating Radio Beacon), which would send our exact position via satellite to some nice people in Falmouth. They would hopefully alert the closest vessel, bearing in mind we would mostly be beyond the range of rescue helicopter help. We demonstrated that we had everything that was needed and that it was all in good order. We passed the safety inspection, subject to making one or two tweaks. That was the biggest 'up' of the day.

One of those necessary tweaks required concerned our tricolour navigation light at the top of the mast. The previous night we had noticed that it was not working properly, so the dress flags had to come down and the halyard that had been used to haul them up the mast was reattached to my brother to haul him up in their place. Robin and I took up positions at the foot of the mast, controlling the halyard and an additional safety line. After a couple of such visits to the masthead, the tricolour was repaired. The halyard and safety lines were then detached from Chris and reattached to the dress flags. Soon they were flying high again and all was well.

A little later, two guys arrived for the second inspection of the day. They had come to check the standing rigging, that is, the ten thick wire shrouds that hold the mast in place. The inspection was organised and paid for by the company that insured the boat. Given what we were doing, the insurers wanted to satisfy themselves that the boats they covered were in the best possible shape to face the rigours of ocean crossing. And so the flags came down again, and the halyard and safety line reattached to a rigger to haul him up the mast.

Chris was not at all apprehensive about this inspection for the simple reason that he had paid a handsome four-figure sum to have the entire rigging on Second Wind renewed just two years earlier in Greece.

It is hard to describe the sudden sense of desolation we all felt when the rigger, apologising profusely for being the bearer of bad news, told us that eight out of the ten shrouds had not been installed properly and would have to be renewed. He tried his best to console us by telling us how many other boats in the marina needed rig repairs, including a brand new top-of-the-range yacht that had failed the inspection, and another boat that he, as the rigger put it, "would not sail to the fuel pontoon." But that only compounded our fears that, with so many other calls on their time, the local rigging business would not be able to deal with us before the ARC start. The unthinkable crossed our minds that, after everything we had been through, we may not after all be able to compete; that was devastating. We did not feel like flying the flags again and so they remained down.

Eventually, later that evening, the proprietor of the local riggers came aboard to see for himself what needed to be done and to assess whether or not the mast would have to be taken down in the process, which really would have been a show-stopper. The news was mixed. The good news was that he was confident the job could be done where the boat was moored, without the need to take it to a boatyard to have the mast removed. The less-good news was that the spoons (so called, no doubt, because they looked nothing like spoons) that connected the shrouds to the mast were not common and would have to be ordered in from Barcelona.

To us, this was yet another potential obstacle that could derail our plans, but the proprietor was confident that the spoons would be delivered without much of a delay, and that his firm would be able to do the work in good time for us to be at the rally start line with everyone else. The cost, however, would be another four-figure sum! Chris was understandably annoyed that the Greek firm had taken him for a ride, but we urged him to see that he had done a noble thing by, single-handedly, bringing forward the recovery of the ailing Greek economy by several months at a stroke. We all felt cheered that our hopes of sailing were still alive, so we reattached the halyard to the signal flags and raised them once again. So the day of ups and downs ended on an up.

Excitement mounts

"I have never seen anything like this in all my life. The excitement is growing so much I think the Geiger counter of Olympomania is going to go zoink off the scale!" (Boris Johnson, Mayor of London, Hyde Park Olympic ceremony, 26th July 2012)

Over the next few days, more and more ARC yachts and crews arrived and the sense of excitement continued to mount. It would be overstating things beyond measure to say that it was just like the 2012 Olympics, but it is fair to say that those excited words of Boris Johnson, our colourful clown of London town, could have equally applied to the ARC opening ceremony on Sunday, 17th November.

The 2013 ARC Rally had attracted yachts registered in 27 different countries and the 1,208 crew members comprised 38 nationalities. It was truly a global event and, in Olympic style, the opening ceremony snaked around the marina perimeter. All the participants grouped behind their national flags, each carried by one of their countrymen, nominated for the honour. The large national flags had been provided by the ARC team who had clearly envisaged that the Scots, Welsh, Northern Irish and English would all group together behind the red, white and blue of the Union Flag. Mostly we did, except a few of the Scottish contingent clearly pre-empted the independence vote of 2014 and had brought their own St Andrew's flag to rally behind. It was strange to think that the famous red, white and blue might have to become just the red and white after the vote, which would be a blue day in my humble opinion.

As hundreds of us paraded along the perimeter of the marina, flags waving, hundreds more watched us pass by. The local police cleared our path and the parade was topped and tailed by two bands; a traditional brass band at the front and a far from traditional core of drums bringing up the rear, their infectious enthusiasm and impressive rhythmic skills injecting pace and energy into the proceedings.

We all rallied at the sea wall adjacent to the marina entrance to hear dignitaries from both sides of the ocean give speeches of encouragement. Although I did not catch his name, the representative from Saint Lucia gave a speech that even Boris Johnson would have been proud to deliver, full of passion, humour and enthusiasm, promising us the warmest of welcomes when we arrived at his country. The flags of each nation represented were then hoisted high and the ceremony brought to an end with the ground-shaking sound of thunder-flashes bursting above our heads. And so we entered the last week before the off.

Arrival and survival

Mid-week saw the arrival of Angela and Jane, the wives of Chris and Robin. They had booked an apartment close by the marina and had come to cheer us on our way. They did that in two ways. They would literally cheer us when the Sunday start came around, but in the meantime, they cheered us by bringing with them many edible treats for us to take on our travels, including Christmas cake, mince pies, stolen, golden-syrup cakes and something for which we had searched the supermarkets of Las Palmas high and low but in vain – Branston pickle! They were most welcome (the ladies and their gifts), although we did not see them for as long as we might have done. That was because these particular two ladies were unashamedly more interested in sales than sails, and Las Palmas offered them a huge array of boutiques and malls to provide the retail therapy they were craving.

Glyn needed therapy of a different kind. He had been struggling with a bad back for the past few weeks and we could all see the difficulty he was having, moving about the boat. Finally, and wisely, he booked some treatment from a local osteopath, the ARC office pointing him in the right direction. The therapy seemed to work as, afterwards, Glyn moved about with increasing ease and confidence.

With Glyn back from the clinic and the ladies fully occupied in the city, Chris got us together to fulfil another one of the ARC's sensible requirements; the skipper's safety briefing. Although we had passed the safety inspection, that was more about having the right equipment to hand and demonstrating that it was all in good order; the briefing was to ensure that we all knew how and when to use it.

In reality, it was not so much a briefing as a discussion about what to do in the event of various survival scenarios. For example, we discussed what we might do should our rudder be lost. Our emergency tiller, which I have mentioned before, may have been the cleanest in the fleet but it was not magic. It could only bypass the linkage between the helm and the rudder such that, if the wheel could not turn the rudder, the emergency tiller would. But what if the rudder itself had gone? Then the emergency tiller, however shiny, would only be turning a stick protruding from the hull. Useless.

One option we discussed was to learn from the ancient mariners and how they steered their boats long before rudders were invented. For them, steering was by means of a wide board attached to a rod, like a broad oar. This was secured to the side of the ship such that the board was held in the water and could be moved by a handle fixed to the rod. As most sailors were right-handed, those crude steering mechanisms were always fixed to the right side of boats. Remember that, in bygone times, the side of a boat was also called a board and so the Old English word 'steobord' came into use, literally meaning the side on which the ship was steered, being the right side. With the passing of time, steobord became starboard.

In order to prevent those steering mechanisms from being damaged against rough quaysides or harbour walls, skippers would always moor their boats so that the left side of the vessel was against the quay or wall. It was because of this practice that left-side became port-side in sailor-speak. The fog of marine language was beginning to clear for me, although I still do not understand why windows on the starboard side of a ship are called port holes.

One way we could have replicated that ancient way of steering would be to attach a board to a pole and find a way to hold it and rotate it under water. We pointed out to Chris that Second Wind's beautifully polished mahogany cupboard doors were an ideal size for such a board, and could easily be taken off and fixed to something like a boathook just by drilling a few holes through them. That suggestion, however, did not prove popular with Chris and so we moved on to plan B.

That plan centred on deploying sea anchors, known as drogues, either side of the boat. Sea anchors are a single or a series of fabric funnels on a line, the large hole at the front and the small hole at the rear. As water streams through the large end and then struggles to exit through the small end, it creates a drag on the vessel, slowing it down. If the drogue is deployed on the port side then the drag effect will make the vessel steer left, and if on the starboard side, the boat will steer right. It would be a very crude and unwieldy steering mechanism but better than nothing.

In theory, the same could be achieved with buckets towed on lanyards, but a word to the wise; the handle on the average builder's bucket is not designed to take such a strain. The best thing to do is to remove the manufacturer's handle and replace it with a rope handle inserted through two holes drilled in the bucket itself. Otherwise, within seconds of deploying your steering buckets, you will find that you are simply towing two bucket handles through the water. That may make you laugh but will certainly not make you turn. Altering bucket handles in this way makes them far more robust even if you do not intend using them for steering. It was certainly one of the jobs we did during our times of preparation.

Another aspect of our safety discussions was to ensure we all knew how to deploy the brand-new life-raft, should that ever become necessary. We reminded ourselves of the marine maxim that we should only step up into our life-raft and never down onto it. In other words, unless there was some other threat to life such as fire, our chances of survival would be increased if we stayed aboard Second Wind until she was literally sinking beneath our feet. The wisdom of this was reinforced by another tragic yachting disaster, the aftermath of which did much to re-write the rules of sea safety and survival.

It happened in 1979. The famous biennial Fastnet race was three days underway when the fleet of over 300 yachts was hit by a fierce storm, which would claim the lives of 15 crew and 3 rescuers. In that frightening maelstrom of wind and waves, 24 yachts were abandoned. In the cold light of day, it was found that only 5 of those abandoned vessels sank; the other 19, although battered and broken, remained afloat and, with the massive benefit of hindsight, would have provided a better haven for their crews. Sadly, 7 of the fatalities occurred amongst those who had abandoned to their life-rafts.

Although the Fastnet disaster highlighted the danger of abandoning ship too soon, knowledge of that danger has been known from way back. Daniel Defoe's classic, Robinson Crusoe, was written in 1719. Fearing shipwreck, the story tells us, 11 people took to a small boat in a vain attempt to row to shore, but the boat was overwhelmed in the storm and all 10 of Robinson Crusoe's companions were drowned, leaving RC alone on the island. The next day, Robinson was walking along the shore of his new island-home and, as written by Defoe, the story reads:

"A little after Noon I found the Sea very calm, and the Tyde ebb'd so far out, that I could come within a Quarter of a Mile of the Ship; and here I found a fresh renewing of my Grief, for I saw evidently, that if we had kept on board, we had been all safe, that is to say, we had all got safe on Shore, and I had not been so miserable as to be left entirely destitute of all Comfort and Company, as now I was..." (Robinson Crusoe)

It was not clear to me why, back in the 1700s, so many capital letters had to be inserted mid-sentence, but it was clear that the notion of not taking to the lifeboats until the main ship is all but lost has been well understood for at least the last three hundred years.

The third scenario we considered was what to do in the event of the mast snapping and coming down. We were, of course, already minimising that risk by having the shrouds renewed (again!) but our mast could still be under threat if the wind became strong and we were to have too much sail exposed to it. The weight of wind in a big sail is unimaginable and would either knock the boat over or be too much even for the brand new shrouds to hold; one or two of them would snap and the mast would topple.

We agreed that the greater danger was not so much having our mast in the water, but that most of the shrouds would still be attached, preventing it from floating away. Instead, those shrouds could hold the mast at right-angles to the boat. As the waves crash in, the mast would then act like a battering ram and, sooner or later, would puncture a hole through the hull below the waterline. Our priority, should we be dismasted, would be to protect the hull by cutting through as quickly as possible any shrouds that were still holding the mast against the side of our boat. Second Wind's safety equipment included heavy-duty bolt croppers for that very purpose.

It seemed ludicrous to be contemplating the ruin of the brand new shrouds that were so expensive and still being fitted up on deck while we were having our discussions in the saloon below. But such scenario planning was not cloud-cuckoo land – at least one of the ARC yachts in the upcoming rally would indeed be dismasted, and another would lose the top section of its mast. Those things do happen to some people and those 'some people' could one day be us.

Finally, Chris checked that we all knew how to use the radios to send a distress call if that were needed. We all hoped of course that we would never have to, but at least, being part of a big rally, there should be yachts not too far distant that could come to our rescue in an emergency. That reminds me of a joke that we were told by a couple from another yacht at one of the ARC pre-rally events (thanks, Loftus and Lyndy). They told us that we had to hope that any Mayday we sent was not picked up by a German crew. If it was, the conversation could well be along the lines of:

"Mayday, Mayday, we are sinking, we are sinking!"

"Zat is good, vot are you sinking about?"

I, of course, would not tell such a joke, so I urge you not to repeat it! However, returning swiftly to the right side of the political correctness line, our survival discussions ended with the arrival of the ladies, back from the shops and eager to show us the contents of many posh-looking carrier bags! Perhaps those shrouds were not so expensive after all.

Final reparations, preparations and celebrations

Undoubtedly one of the highlights of the final week was seeing those riggers working on the shrouds. The rigging proprietor was as good as his word and the job, although spread over four days as they tried to juggle the needs of all their customers, was completed two full days before the rally start. It was like a dark cloud being lifted. We had all wanted to believe that the work would be done in time but there was always a nagging doubt lurking in the depths of our minds. Now those doubts had been dispersed and we knew for certain that we would take our place in Sunday's start, along with all the other competitors. All bar one, that is. Unfortunately for one crew, their dark cloud was never lifted; a problem with their keel could not be sorted and their rally was over before it had started. We felt for them.

There was not a great deal left for us to do in that final week except on the food front. We ordered our fresh fruit and vegetables from the local market and prepared a quartet of curries and chilli-con-carnes to see us through the first few days of sailing. While shopping, we also completed the upgrade of Second Wind's first aid kit with the purchase of a course of the antibiotic, erythromycin, for each of us; this was the general antibiotic that had been recommended to us at our First Aid course.

Doctors we had spoken with back in England were unable rather than unwilling to provide such antibiotics just on the off-chance that one of us, or indeed all of us, might need them at some future point. However, the rules were different in the Canaries and a simple letter from Chris, as a ship's skipper, was sufficient for the pills to be supplied. We still hoped of course that we would not need them, or have call to open the first aid box at all, although Robin did need a plaster when he somehow managed to stab himself on the end of a guitar string!

Glyn devoted some of his time to the honing of his bread-baking skills, experimenting with different types of flour and other ingredients. Unhappy as he was with the first few, his later loaves looked and tasted very good indeed and he would go on to bake a loaf for us most days of our ocean voyage. Robin, meanwhile, took time to uprate his fishing tackle, having been convinced by a number of people that the fish he was likely to catch could well be bigger than he thought and beyond the breaking strain of his original line. And all the time, Chris pottered about like a modern-day Caractacus Potts, tools in hand, tinkering with anything and everything.

Helpful seminars

During those final days, we attended three ARC-organised seminars. One was on the night sky, its aim being to help us identify some of the wonders of the universe that we would be seeing, as well as alerting us as to when and where to look to see an expected comet and a likely meteor shower. We were also encouraged to watch out for an atmospheric phenomenon whereby a sunset could be immediately followed by either a green flash or sometimes green streaks radiating upwards into the dusk. We were told that the uninterrupted view of the horizon that our ocean sailing would provide was the best platform to witness this wonder.

If you cannot easily visualise what I am talking about, you could watch the final film in the Pirates of the Caribbean series, titled At World's End; it features this green flash a couple of times. I can tell you now that we were never to see even a glimmer of green during the rally, but the fact that our looking for it made us fix our eyes on many a glorious sunset was prize enough.

Another of the seminars was on the weather and the recommended route to take in the light of it. In particular, we were taught how to identify Atlantic squalls and what to do before they hit us, as hit us they most certainly would. We were told of the two main dangers of squalls. The serious one was that the wind speed could and would literally double within seconds, and so our sails would need to be reefed as soon as we realised that we were on a collision course with such a squall.

The not-so-serious second danger was viewing a squall as a welcome opportunity in the heat of the tropics to take a freshwater shower in its heavy rain. Our tutor told us that many a crew member on past rallies had stripped off and lathered up only to find that the rain stopped as quickly as it started, catching out the soapy dopes before they had time to rinse off the suds. Attempting such showers was not deemed the best of boating practice but might possibly win the ARC's competition for the best photograph taken at sea.

Provisioning was the topic of the third seminar, which was attended only by Glyn in his victualling role. There he picked up the recommendation that all foodstuffs should be taken out of their cardboard containers before going on board, as cockroaches lay their eggs in cardboard. We did follow this rule as far as practicable, and yet a couple of the critters still found their way on board somehow. They may have had pretensions to become our room-mates but we quickly turned them into flat mates.

Glyn also advised, following the seminar, that all fresh produce should be washed and dried, and some even individually wrapped either in paper or foil, before being stowed. He had arranged for our fresh food to be delivered from the local market on the final Friday. A small mountain of fruit and vegetables duly arrived and Glyn and I set about washing each piece individually and laying them out on the rear deck to dry. By the time we had finished, the back of Second Wind was a riot of colour and looked just like a traditional Harvest Festival display; others on our pontoon paused to admire and photograph it, and one even mistook us for a greengrocers, asking if he could buy some apples from us.

"Events, dear boy, events." (Harold Macmillan, Prime Minister, 1957-1963)

Harold Macmillan gave this response when asked what it was he most feared. While politicians today still fear 'events', because they interrupt the smooth running of governments, I believe when it comes to the annual ARC rally, it is the other way around; it is not events that are feared but rather, because there are fears lurking, events are arranged to help quell them. I am guessing a bit here, but I am sure that it is because those at the World Cruising Club are very aware of nervousness setting in amongst first-time participants that they go to the lengths they do to organise so many events. The formal seminars no doubt played their part in addressing some of our specific concerns, but the many other social events were all brilliantly diversionary. They included dinners, barbeques, outings, parties and, of course, the daily Sundowners.

The Sundowners are a good example of what I am saying.

They continued to attract the majority of participants each evening and it was really good to have those regular get-togethers organised for us. However, as we got closer to the rally start, it became increasingly obvious that, beneath the happy banter, some people were beginning to feel apprehensive and a few even quite fearful.

Making matters worse was a man at one of the last Sundowner events repeatedly laughing and joking about all the injuries and incidents suffered on previous ARC rallies. He was the proverbial 'spectre at the feast', bringing to people's minds the thoughts they least wanted to think. Not surprisingly, he had never done the Atlantic passage himself, nor was he about to do it, and so I guess he should be forgiven for not realising that his being there that day was depriving some village of an idiot. His input was the last thing wanted by those who felt as nervous as a long-tailed cat in a room full of rocking chairs. But he was the exception, and the mutual support and encouragement of the Sundowners, and all the other ARC events, went a long way to dispel people's fears.

Party fever!

We on Second Wind enjoyed punctuating our preparations with no fewer than four parties. The first was sponsored by the main chandlers, no doubt as a thank-you for the way ARC competitors had worn out their cash-register over recent days. The live music and free food was a winning formula. The chandler's staff were there in force, although their drinking and dancing was often interrupted by some skippers still looking for help and advice as to how to mend bits and pieces on their yachts before the off.

The second party was the wig party. Chris, Robin and I had packed wigs that we happened to have at home, harking back to 1960s hairstyles. We thought they made us look ridiculous and it was hard to accept that they simply made us look like what we once really did look like! Glyn did not have a wig in his fancy dress box at home and so he made his own on the day, cleverly unravelling a rope into its single strands and sewing them into the rim of an old hat. We must have all looked very peculiar but thankfully unrecognisable as we walked the short distance to the event. Fortunately, we had got the day right and were soon amongst many others who looked equally odd. I confess that the music that night went on for much longer than we did, its beat still audible from our beds at four o'clock the following morning.

Next was the 'fantasy world' fancy dress event for which we had designed and purchased those specially-printed T-shirts with what we hoped were the winning words across our chests. I would love to be able to tell you that we won on the night but I cannot. Regrettably, the slow-service of a local restaurant delayed us and we arrived at the party just as the host was announcing the fancy dress winners! Never mind. Our costumes still amused many there, so it was worth the effort.

The last party was an extravaganza of a do, sponsored by the Gran Canaria Tourist Board and held on the waterfront premises of a nearby exclusive sailing club. Great food was served, together with rum punch to give crews an early taste of that Caribbean favourite. The entertainment was spectacular. Fireworks banged and boomed above us as we ate, lighting up the night sky and being perfectly mirrored in the sea below. We were then serenaded by bands, including the core of drummers that had impressed so much at the opening ceremony. Their repeat performance was just as remarkable, their pounding resounding around the harbour. After that it was the turn of the dancers to put on a show, all bangled and spangled in flamboyantly exotic costumes, replete with frills and feathers. Another great evening, enjoyed by all.

Just as the event was finishing, we were given a quick reminder of how cold and wet an Atlantic squall can be, as one was suddenly upon us, but it did not dampen our spirits as we made our way back to our boat. All the parties were wonderful in their different ways, and added greatly to the carnival atmosphere that characterises the ARC way of doing things.

"I am in the most magnificent health and spirits, eating like a bull, sleeping like a tree, yet I shall not enjoy a moment till I hear my old tarpaulins tramping round the capstan. Seaward ho!" (Squire Trelawney, Treasure Island)

Like Squire Trelawney before us, we were in good health and good spirits, sleeping well at night and enjoying ourselves immensely during the day. But now we were beginning to feel like the Squire did in his Treasure Island role. In that most famous of stories, he had spent long weeks overseeing the preparation of the ship Hispaniola, readying it to search for hidden treasure, but he had reached that point when he just wanted to put to sea, and so had we. Being a Squire, he had tarpaulins to winch up his anchor and sails for him, tarpaulins being the olde worlde term for sailors, later shortened to 'tars'.

We, on the other hand, were not Squires and so we would have to do our own hauling and winching, but we were now more than keen to do it and go. Seaward ho!

Chapter Five

Seaward ho!

Approaching the start

"What we think, or what we know, or what we believe is, in the end, of little consequence. The only consequence is what we do." (John Ruskin, 1819-1900)

24th November 2013 dawned, the rally start day. More than a year had passed since my brother's invitation for me to be part of the adventure of a lifetime. During that year, the four of us had done our best to prepare the yacht and ourselves. But that was all now history, and John Ruskin's timeless words came to mind. We thought we were ready, we knew how to sail, we believed we would make it, but all of that was of little consequence. Now was the day for doing the thing.

Whatever the outcome would be, we had the satisfaction of knowing that we had already scored a morale-boosting victory over one of the racing crews. It happened during the previous evening. As you might imagine, being the eve of the rally start, all the nearby restaurants had been fully booked. Just one, however, had a single outside table that could not be reserved and was allocated on a first come, first served basis. We had learned about this and had been briskly walking towards that restaurant, aiming to be standing outside their door a few minutes before they opened.

A crew of racers had the same idea and they were walking just as briskly towards the same restaurant, coming from the opposite direction. We spotted them before they spotted us;

it was a fair race and we won it! Before the doors opened, we had to listen to them talk about how their yacht was faster than the wind itself, but at least we proved that we were more fleet of foot than they were! Our evening meal tasted that much sweeter in the light of such a victory, setting us up nicely for the day ahead.

We would be following in the famous footsteps of Christopher Columbus. In 1492, he like us had never sailed the Atlantic Ocean, and he like us was to set off from the Canaries where he had stopped for running repairs (perhaps his rigging had been installed in Greece). We hoped that would be the end of the similarities. His voyage took him five weeks whereas we hoped to do it in three or four at the most. He arrived at the Bahamas but was convinced it was Asia, whereas we had satellite navigation. And whereas we fully expected to be eating Christmas Dinner on terra firma, his ship ran aground and sank off Haiti on Christmas Day 1492. I wonder if his unfortunate mishap was because he had changed the name of his ship from Marigalante to Santa Maria, not knowing it was unlucky to do so?

The official reason given was that only a cabin boy was at the helm, with Christopher and crew celebrating Christmas down below, and all being 'three sheets to the wind'. This is a nautical expression I now understand. You may recall that sheets are the ropes that control the sails, so three of them flying in the wind indicates the ship is not under control, lurching from side to side like a drunkard, hence the phrase means so drunk as to be falling over. If Columbus had been just tipsy, he would have been only one sheet to the wind on the sailors' sliding scale of drunkenness. This scale is well described in the 1824 novel 'The Fisher's Daughter', which includes the line, "Wolf replenished his glass at the request of Mr. Blust, who, instead of being one sheet in the wind, was likely to get to three before he took his departure."

We, however, were to be no sheets in the wind when we took our departure. We had already decided in our planning meetings that Second Wind would be an almost dry boat, alcohol free except for the odd bottle of wine or champagne to celebrate significant milestones in our Atlantic crossing, such as reaching the half-way point. We did have additional alcohol but that was primarily reserved for fish. Robin had learned from others that spraying alcohol into the gills of a caught fish kills it rather more sedately than whanging it on the head with a winch handle, and I guess may also help to marinade it at the same time.

As the morning passed, we said our good-byes to Angela and Jane, took down the signal flags for the last time this side of the ocean, secured the Red Ensign to the stern and did our last-minute checks to ensure we were ready to go. We also received the first Fleet Report, a daily email that would be issued from the ARC office giving us a weather summary and other news while we were at sea. The first report included an alert that a red semi-submerged container had been spotted on the route south.

These containers are an increasing menace to small craft. Estimates of how many of them are lost at sea each year vary widely from high hundreds to a figure nearer 10,000, more than one every hour of the night and day. I am sure that the day will come when the Channel Tunnel is no longer needed because people will be able to walk to France across a bridge of bobbing containers.

The fact that these steel boxes do not sink, sometimes for

months on end, is the real problem. It is widely accepted that, tragically, they have caused the loss of lives as well as boats at sea. It is hard to find anything favourable to say about them except perhaps that, unintentionally, these floating hazards are helping oceanographers gain a better understanding of ocean currents. Also, the loss of one specific container back in 1992 helped a guy called Donovan Hohn write an amusing book by the title of Moby-Duck. The container spilled some 28,800 durable rubber bath toys into the ocean and Donovan made it his life's work to track them down.

We're off!

At 11.25 GMT we slipped our moorings and joined the procession of ARC yachts making its way out through the marina entrance to the cheers, applause and camera flashes of many folk who had come to see the spectacle. And it was spectacular. Sailing boats of every description were on the move, the newest being brand new and the oldest dating back to 1921 although, sadly, that lovely 93 year old boat would not complete the rally but would have to take refuge in Barbados following a fire aboard. I suppose if you have to take refuge somewhere, Barbados is as nice a place as any.

To put this procession into perspective, if all the ARC yachts were placed end-to-end they would have stretched for 1.8 nautical miles, not counting the many spectator boats that weaved their way among us. Of course, with so many yachts taking part, there was always a danger that a couple of them may be placed end-to-end actually rather than figuratively. In view of this, we all had to tie a fender over whatever protruded the furthest from our bows, normally the anchor or a bowsprit, to protect anything we might inadvertently hit in such crowded seas.

The event was on such a scale that the whole Port of Las Palmas de Gran Canaria was brought to an arranged standstill, allowing the mid-morning start to proceed unhindered by other shipping. A Spanish Navy vessel controlled the start line and counted us down to the start time by the firing of a canon. The racers, as always, started first to avoid us slow-boats getting in the way of their attempts to break records. But then it was our turn; the final canon fired and we were off!

Over the radio we heard the ARC Control congratulate the fleet on a clean start, except for two yachts that had crossed the line a little early and would suffer a time penalty as a consequence. The radio voice then added, "And if you have not looked behind you, I suggest you do." We did, and ominous black clouds were scudding across the sky and heading straight for us.

The spirit of the ARC shines through the clouds

We were sure that the folk back home would be imagining us in shorts and T-shirts under an azure blue sky. The reality was we were in our full foul-weather gear for good reason; it was foul weather! The black sky was soon above us, the rain upon us, and the wind had picked up considerably. We also knew that the wind would strengthen even further as we made our way down the east side of Gran Canaria, that corridor of sea being a well-known wind acceleration zone. But despite being cold, wet and windswept, we were enjoying it. We had waited so long for this day and now we were on our way.

After an hour or so in those stormy conditions, we heard a fellow-competitor attempt to call the ARC Control over the VHF radio. There was no response. He tried twice more, but still without reply. Then another yacht radioed him and, for me, that call epitomised the whole spirit of the ARC. He said, "It seems the ARC Control has closed down its radio but the whole fleet is here with you. Can any of us help you?"

As it happened, none of us could help. The yacht had suffered a broken boom in the strong winds and had no option but to return to Las Palmas for repairs, but how reassuring it was to have that timely reminder that we were not alone. What better advertisement was there to encourage would-be ocean crossers to do it as part of a rally rather than in splendid isolation, which would become anything but splendid if serious difficulties were encountered. That initial offer of support would not be the last time that yachts in the ARC family would try to help other yachts in difficulties as the days at sea took their toll.

Although we did not need the help of others at that time, we did have our own problem to deal with on that first day. We were winching the genoa sheet, not realising in the dusk that it was caught around the box that housed our generator. The straps that held down the generator box were no match against the strength of the winch and they suddenly snapped under the strain. The box, and generator within it, toppled sideways and slewed across the deck toward the guardrail. Thankfully, it did not go overboard or spill too much fuel, which it so easily could have done. A couple of us leapt forward to prevent its loss and effected a temporary fix until we could secure it more permanently. The generator had been saved and a valuable lesson learned; from then on, we were constantly alert to lines wrapping themselves around the many deck obstacles.

Without further mishap, we sailed into the night. By about midnight, the mast-top navigation lights of only about 20 yachts were visible to us. It amazed us how quickly and widely the fleet had dispersed over just 12 hours or so, each yacht sailing into its own unimpeded space. This surprised us at the time, but later in the rally, we would sail for eight full days and nights without seeing hide nor hair of another yacht, or indeed a vessel of any description. But when you consider that the Atlantic Ocean spans about one fifth of the earth's surface, it should not be so surprising that solitude is the norm. If being neighbourly is not up your street, then ocean sailing could well be for you!

One day down, many more to come

At this point in our story, we had reached the end of our first day at sea. It is tempting to now give a blow-by-blow account of every subsequent day. I shall resist that temptation, as such an account would be mind-numbingly repetitive. Those who know anything about ocean sailing will know that, in the round, some of the things we did on one day, we would do on every day.

For example, the weather forecast was always studied. The sails were always set and continuously adjusted to suit the conditions. The route was always plotted and the helm always manned. Breakfast, lunch and dinner were routinely prepared, eaten and cleared away. We washed and shaved, except on the days that we did not. The log was updated and the odd blog written and emailed. Cat-naps were taken to make up for the loss of sleep due to the night watches. Fishing line and lure were deployed, initially more in hope than expectation.

And we looked. We looked at the sea because it told us so much about the invisible wind. We looked at the sunrises, the sunsets and the stars simply because they were irresistible. We looked at the compass because it told us where we were going, and we looked at our speed instrument to find out how long it would take us to get there. We looked out for squalls because we feared them; we looked out for sealife because it enchanted us; we looked out for other vessels to ensure we avoided them; we looked out for semi-submerged containers just because we knew one was out there somewhere.

Most importantly of all, we looked out for each other because what we were doing was not devoid of danger, and also because, to succeed in the challenge, we had to collaborate, each bringing our strengths to the fore. For example, when berthing the boat in a busy marina, Robin had the edge, whereas Chris had an inventiveness for mending things that was legendary. As for helming, all three of my messmates were skilled and careful, just as I tried to be. For getting the best out of the sails, we looked to Chris and Robin. When it came to answering quiz questions, and we would answer literally hundreds over the course of the rally, Chris and I had to defer to the far wider knowledge of Glyn and Robin on a whole range of topics like history and films, monarchy and music.

When alertness was required first thing in the morning then Chris and I fitted the bill and Robin definitely did not, but his alertness, once it had kicked in, took him through to the small hours of the morning when Chris and I would be all but dead. Nor did Robin profess to be a cook but the other three of us could turn our hand to it pretty well. Chris especially seemed to have the knack of knocking up a meal beyond what the small galley was designed for, although he also earned the reputation, fully deserved, for using every pot, pan, plate and piece of cutlery in the process. But no matter, because Robin was great at washing up! And so it went on.

If a heavy rope needed to be hauled or a weight-filled winch needed winding, then Glyn would freely admit that he was not the man for it, not having quite the upper-body strength of the rest of us. But below stairs, Glyn came into his own, not only baking our daily bread but generally managing our food supplies. When Chris was above deck, checking snap-shackles and knots, Glyn was below deck checking Snap, Crackles and Pops. Both were important.

Glyn also gave a level of after-sales care to fruit and vegetables that was touching. In fact, it was literally touching as, day by day, he would inspect each piece of fruit and every vegetable, gently turning each one to ensure even ripening and so extend its shelf-life. Glyn does not have kids of his own but if he did, we were convinced he would name his sons something like Chip, or Spud, and his daughters would have to be Cherry or Clementine. But seriously, it was in no small measure down to Glyn's fastidiousness on our behalf that we would still be eating fresh fruit and vegetables at the end of this long rally, to which I shall now return, not noting every detail of every day but sharing just a few memorable things in the order in which they occurred.

25th November (Day 2) An unexpected guest

The weather was not playing ball. The predicted trade winds had been interrupted by a depression and we were still in need of our foul-weather gear. Suddenly, as if from nowhere, a racing pigeon landed in our cockpit and showed no signs of wanting to leave, perhaps sheltering from the wet and blustery conditions. It was very tame, not seeming to mind a bit when we picked it up and placed it more out of the way, next to our instrument panel. His arrival concerned us much more than it concerned him. Chris especially had an aversion to birds in enclosed spaces, and birds seemed to sense it. As a boy, he had once refused to go into the bird house of a zoo, believing it was wiser and safer to wait outside. When the rest of the family emerged, we saw that a passing bird had left a personal present on the top of his head; he never fully recovered from that childhood trauma!

As the day and night unfolded, the wind strength had progressively increased to some 20 knots blowing over our stern. That was more like what we had expected, and our boat-speed picked up considerably. The sea state, however, made Second Wind roll severely all night, causing a flying fish incident. The flying fish in question were not the live variety but our entire supply of tinned fish, which flew across the saloon and sprawled over the floor when the roll of the boat caused one of our cupboard doors to spring open. Something else happened during the night; something that we had all wondered whether it would ever happen – we overtook one of the ARC yachts!

26th November (Day 3) A day to look back

Since the time I unpacked my holdall, an unopened envelope had been by my bed. It had been secretly inserted in my luggage by Maureen and this was the day for opening it because it was our wedding anniversary; the first that we had spent apart. Allow me just a couple of sentences to pay tribute to my dear wife. I still pinch myself when I think back to a day when a shy 17 year old girl stood in a church and committed herself to me, not just for weeks or months or even years, but for the rest of her life. That was now 36 years ago, and every day since I have watched her keeping the promises she made. I am not sure that I recognise every blessing that comes my way, but I certainly recognise that one!

To celebrate, I had sneaked on board the ingredients for a special celebratory lunch, including Canarian Potatoes – boiled new potatoes smothered with a warm Mojo sauce; delicious! Unfortunately, Robin was not there to enjoy it. He had taken to his bed suffering sea-sickness, poor chap. When the seas heave, so do some people, and Robin happens to be one of them. We knew this would keep him low for a couple of days at least.

His spirits were not much lifted even when we told him that another crew had caught a 15 pound bluefin tuna. We discovered this by tuning into the daily ARC radio net at noon. The ARC net was a really useful, regular radio link up with those yachts around us that were within VHF range. Volunteers took turns in hosting the daily calls. Not all the news, though, was encouraging. We learned that another yacht had developed serious leaks and was returning to Las Palmas, its rally over.

The wind of the previous two days had all but disappeared and the weather forecast was dismaying, with no wind predicted for at least two days more. Our ultimate destination was due west but because there was likely to be more of a breeze if we stayed closer to the coast of Africa, we kept heading south towards the west side of the Cape Verde Islands, which are about 350 miles off the west coast of Africa. We discovered later that some boats elected to stay even closer to the African coastline, skirting round the east side of the islands in their scavenge for wind.

At least the rain had been replaced with sunshine and the sea was calm, and although we would routinely see dolphins throughout our voyage, this was the first time that we saw them propel themselves out of the water vertically and pirouette on their tails. Amazing! Staying with wildlife, our resident pigeon was making quite a mess in the corner of our cockpit so we concluded that the time for eviction had come. I launched it into the sky, hoping it would find a new home. It did. It circled around for a few seconds and then decided that our solar panel gantry was to be its new place to stay! We began to think of pigeon pie.

27th November (Day 4) A burial at sea

This was a difficult day. The latest forecast predicted little wind for at least the next three days. We were going nowhere fast and knew we now had no chance of arriving at Saint Lucia by our target date of 15th December. This had been a purely selfish target. The final Sundowner event of Las Palmas had been sponsored by a sailing club in Saint Lucia and came with the promise of a hog roast on a sun-drenched beach and free rum punch for all crews who could make the crossing by that date. Our lack of progress so far, coupled with the awful forecast, convinced us that a 15th December arrival was now beyond our reach.

We decided to keep heading south, using our engine from time to time, but sparingly. We were not prohibited from using the engine, but the amount of fuel we carried was not sufficient to make much of a dent in such a long overall journey. Additionally, any engine hours would incur time penalties under the ARC handicap system. Our new plan was to make for the Cape Verde Islands and perhaps even sit it out there until the normal trade winds kicked in again. To reach those islands in such fickle winds would take us another five days of sailing at least. No wind is a killer both to speed and morale. Those windless days would be for us the most mentally challenging of the whole crossing. We were learning the hard way that the romance of the sea and the reality of the sea were sometimes poles apart.

The calm seas did, however, allow us to carry out one important ceremony. One of the last things Chris had done before leaving Las Palmas was to buy a new outboard engine for the dinghy, as the old one was nearing the end of its usefulness. But, and this may sound bizarre at first, Chris did not want to simply throw the old engine into a skip, preferring instead to give it a serious and solemn burial at sea. Why, you may ask? It was all to do with not wanting to upset his son, Jon, who is the younger of my brother's two children.

Jon had not been happy with his dad's choice of 'Second Wind' as the new name for the yacht so, to appease him, Chris had invited Jon to choose a new name for the yacht's rubber dinghy. Cheered by this, Jon overlooked the obvious name of 'Second Thoughts' and christened the dinghy 'Nautilus'. As part of that renaming process, he had repainted the old outboard a bright blue, stencilled the new name on it, and referred to himself as Captain Nemo every time he used it. Chris therefore wanted to dispose of the old engine sensitively, and send pictures back to Jon, hence the idea of a formal burial at sea was born. And this was as good a time as any.

The old engine was laid gently to rest on the now-removed gangplank, or passerelle to give it its posh name. It was then covered with a Red Ensign attached to the plank at one end to allow the engine to slip out from under it at the appropriate time. Next, the yacht's sound system was primed with the Royal Marines Band playing Abide With Me, interspersed with The Last Post played on the bugle. As the music played, my brother and I lifted the plank to the side of the boat and I said some words, assuring the outboard that it would not grow old as we that are left grow old; age would not weary it, nor the years condemn; and at the going down of the sun and in the morning, we would remember it. We then tilted up the back of the passerelle and the engine slipped gracefully into the water. Nothing could have been more dignified.

Glyn videoed the proceedings and Robin took a number of still photographs, some of which were immediately sent home for Jon to see. We hoped he was not too upset. Jon, by the way, is 24 and aiming to become an airline pilot. Saints preserve us!

We would never know whether our resident pigeon was overcome by the emotion of the whole thing but it suddenly stretched its wings and was off, never to be seen by us again. We were happy to see it go and immediately disinfected where it had been and, more specifically, where it had *been*. However, we would probably tell Jon that the spirit of Nautilus had obviously entered into the pigeon and he had carried it up to that great marina in the sky where all broken engines end their days in happy revving.

28th November (Day 5) A fish arrived

Our first fish was caught. Strictly speaking, it just arrived rather than us catching it. It was a sizeable flying fish. Over the coming days we would see literally hundreds of these remarkable fish breaking the sea surface and fizzing away from the bow of the boat at tremendous speed, possibly mistaking us for a predator. To be fair, we would have been a predator if we could have caught any of them, happily turning them from flying fish into frying fish. But they were far too fast and elusive for us. Incredibly, these amazing creatures can reach speeds of about 40 miles per hour. The combination of their unusually large pectoral fins, torpedo-shaped bodies and tails that flap amazingly rapidly, enables them to stay above the surface for long distances.

I have seen a YouTube clip showing a flying fish fizzing above the surface for a full 45 seconds. However, the fish that visited us was presumably the only one of its kind in the whole Atlantic Ocean with myopia. It had over 41,000,000 square miles of ocean to play with, virtually obstacle-free, yet crash-landed on our deck; its final flight.

The mood on board remained sombre as our progress was very slow. Every now and again, a wind of sorts began to blow, but within minutes, die away again. This was not what we had signed up for. If Doctor Who was real and could have time-travelled us to somewhere else, I think we would have taken him up on it, especially Robin, whose increasingly-sought-after sons were playing the iconic Brixton Academy that night. Understandably, he would have loved to have been there with them. Being away from home for so long required sacrifices to be made that sometimes were not easy to bear. We were cheered a little when the largest pod of dolphins we had seen so far came to play with us, dozens of them leaping and darting in all directions. Just as ocean-sailing has its downs, it has its ups too, and watching dolphin displays was one of them.

29ᵗʰ November (Day 6) Our woes put into perspective

The day started well. A fairly strong wind came to help us. It had not been forecast, neither was it the trade wind we longed for, but it did enable good sailing for a few hours. All too soon, however, the wind again petered out to almost nothing. That was not the worst of it. According to Edward Lear's famous poem, it was The Jumblies who "...went to sea in a sieve, they did. In a sieve they went to sea." Not surprisingly, the poem goes on to say, "The water it soon came in, it did. The water it soon came in." I am not suggesting that Second Wind was a sieve, but a trickle of water did find its way through a window seal.

Ordinarily, it would not have mattered a jot, but those few drops happened to land on our laptop and killed it. Despite our best efforts to dry it out, both in the sunshine and in the oven, it would not work again, and we did not have a spare. That laptop was our only means of downloading detailed wind charts each day; its loss was serious. From that time on, our only access to specific weather information was Angela contacting Chris via the yacht's Yellowbrick tracker, a feature of which enabled messages to be sent and received using the iridium satellite network. Columbus could not do that!

If we thought we had reason to feel sorry for ourselves, it was immediately dispelled at 12.00 noon GMT when the daily ARC radio net announced the truly shocking news that one of the ARC skippers had suffered a suspected heart attack and had died. After hearing such tragic news, nothing else seemed to matter much for a while.

30th November (Day 7) Gales in the sails

We were back in our foul-weather gear and the rain-filled darkness of the early morning hours was frequently interrupted by bright sheet lightning. We did not mind a bit because the wind had returned with a vengeance, gusting at gale force. Better still, it stayed with us for the whole of the day and most of the next night. Our speed rarely dipped below 7 knots. And the pod of dolphins that joined us was even bigger than the one that came to us on the fifth day. Our spirits were lifted again.

1st December (Day 8) Going too fast!

At the speed we were travelling, we would have reached the Cape Verde Islands in the dead of night. As it is always better to arrive somewhere new in daylight (and I cannot believe I am about to say this) we deliberately slowed down, pacing ourselves during the day to delay reaching the islands until the first light of dawn.

2nd December (Day 9) A delightful stopover

We had got the timing right and were approaching the Cape Verde Islands as dawn was breaking. The wind had again died away to nothing. The sunrise was a particularly beautiful one and the early morning light revealed simply stunning scenery. Everything was bathed in soft pinks and purples, the calm seas perfectly reflecting the tinted clouds above. On our starboard side was the large island of Santo Antão, its rugged coastline adding to the dramatic beauty of the overall scene. And once again, the dolphins were with us, which was lovely for us but clearly frightened some of the fish who did their best to impersonate their flying cousins in their attempts to escape becoming dolphin-dinner.

We were heading for the smaller island of São Vicente on our port side, and specifically to the marina on the edge of the ancient city of Mindelo, the second largest city of the island group. The marina was much larger than we had expected. On entering, it was immediately clear that at least 20 other ARC boats were already there. Once moored, we spoke to some other crews about their intentions. Some were staying overnight, others longer, as the elusive trade winds were still awaited and not expected anytime soon. Given the dismal forecast, we decided to at least stay overnight, giving ourselves the day to explore the historic city and the prospect of a good night's sleep without the interruption of a night-watch duty.

That unexpected day in Mindelo was a real bonus; a place we had no plans to visit and, in all likelihood, would never visit again, yet it was charming. Marinas are always deceptive, giving the impression that a well-heeled, leisurely lifestyle is the norm. But beyond the Mindelo marina gates was a city marked with poverty and hard-living. The day was sticky-hot but we had only this one opportunity to explore, and it was well worth the sweat.

The principal buildings reflected the style and grandeur of their old colonial masters (the Portuguese rather than Great Britain in this case, although good old Sir Francis Drake did his best to take the islands over on a couple of occasions). But even their grandest of buildings had suffered the ravages of time, their once brightly painted exteriors fading and the brickwork crumbling with age. The islands had prospered for some 400 years until the 19th century, but after that, they lost their main source of income when it became no longer acceptable to trade in slaves.

Further away from the main square, the buildings were just as colourful but more simple in design, until they became little more than primitive where the city extremes met the surrounding mountains. Near the harbour, open-air markets sold an array of fruits and fish, and many other things too. Most of the markets were not as we know them but were simply places where the locals congregated, bringing with them anything that they might be able to sell.

Local women sat in their doorways offering sweets or home-made biscuits for the equivalent of a few pence. Along the coast-road were huddles of people, some standing around makeshift tables covered in things that had washed up on the beach, and others just sitting on the ground, surrounded by stuff that we would have thrown out long ago, but for which they hoped to find a buyer. And we were those buyers!

Amongst the 'junk' we spotted some second-hand 40 litre plastic containers. Because we were unsure how much fuel we might use in our search for wind to take us across the sea, we bought four of those large containers to fill with diesel and strap to our already overcrowded deck. The price we paid was good for both parties; cheap for us, but more than enough to make the locals cheerful. To be honest, our little transaction did not *make* them cheerful at all. Perhaps I should have said 'to *keep* the locals cheerful' as, from what we could see, the islanders appeared happy and content, despite their lack of the material wealth that seems so important to us in the UK.

Less happy, I suspect, was the owner of another ARC yacht that arrived in the afternoon. It was at least a 50 footer and looked quite new, but its boom was terminally bent and twisted, probably from an uncontrolled or unintentional gybe in the strong winds of the squalls that hit us from time to time. Whatever the cause, something that was worth well over £10,000 before it happened had been instantly reduced to scrap value. The next day it would probably be on one of those makeshift tables along the roadside, the smiling locals hoping to get a few euros for the bits of it they could salvage. And so the world economy continues to grind, based as it always is on 'the rich and the rest'.

As evening came, we decided to give our galley a rest and go out for dinner. We ignored the very plush restaurant that appeared to be part of the marina, opting instead to go back into the city and find a place where the locals ate. We struggled a bit to make ourselves understood but enjoyed the experience as well as the food. Before bed, there was one further bitter-sweet task and that was to phone home; it was sweet to be able to speak to Maureen but the bitter bit was having to tell her that the lack of wind and the abysmal forecast meant that I would almost certainly not be home for Christmas after all.

3rd December (Day 10) A welcome wind

Although no wind had been forecast, we decided to take our chances and leave the Cape Verde Islands as early as we could, but only after filling our newly-acquired containers with contingency diesel; as things turned out, we would not need it, but it gave us peace of mind to have it. We had found out that the fuel pontoon opened each morning at 06.00, which should aid a quick get-away. However, we did not know how many other ARC boats had similar plans, so we got up ridiculously early and, under the cover of darkness, we stealthily slipped our moorings so that we could sneak our boat alongside the fuel pontoon before anyone else was awake, putting ourselves at the front of any fuel queue. But our cunning plan was thwarted by another crew that had got up even earlier. Can no-one be trusted these days? Is there no honour left in the world?

Then it was the turn of the fuel pump itself to dash our plans. The pressure was so weak that a dripping tap could have filled our containers more quickly. The fuel pontoon did indeed open at 06.00 but it was 08.00 by the time sufficient diesel had trickled into our tanks and we could leave, heading out into open water and freeing up the fuel station for the next yacht to pass a frustrating hour or two.

Fortunately for us, there was a slight breeze, which continued to strengthen such that by midday, contrary to the forecasted lull, we had 10 to 15 knots of wind on our beam and enjoyed great sailing well into the night. To add to our encouragement, Robin had two fish nibble at his lure (or possibly the same fish nibbling twice); both escaped but we knew then that it was only a matter of time before fresh fish would be on our menu.

The only other snippet of conversation worth recording from the day concerned Glyn and the wig-hat that he wore at the party back in Las Palmas. After that event, three of us had put our wigs away for ever but Glyn, for some unknown reason, continued to wear his wig at some point during most days, the unravelled rope strands of 'hair' cascading down his back. Chris finally put into words what the other two of us had been thinking:

"Glyn, why do you keep wearing that hat?"

"Why? Don't you like it?"

"I don't care one way or the other, as long as you know it makes you look like a prat."

The wig-hat was not to be seen again.

5th December (Day 12) A cracking day

No sailing had been possible on Day 11 but a light wind had returned, and this time with an important difference. We had had light winds before but this was the first time that it blew from a direction that suited our cruising chute, the sail we had never yet deployed successfully. The change of rig required to fly this chute took us about an hour to effect, as most of our lines had to be re-routed and the new oak bowsprit brought into use. When everything was ready, we hauled up the sail, the breeze filled it and the chute ballooned open. The boat surged forward just as if a turbo-booster had suddenly been activated.

In defence of Chris, most of what he designs and builds works well, but not this time; despite the breeze being light, the weight of wind in the huge chute caused an upward pressure on the bowsprit that was too much even for the century-old oak to take. There was a loud crack as the bowsprit snapped in two, the greater part flying upwards with great force. Had Kate Winslet been standing on our bow at the time, arms outstretched and swooning to the tune of My Heart Will Go On, it would have hit her squarely under the jaw and shut her up for ever. But she wasn't. The good news, however, was that the chute was not damaged and would live to fly another day.

6th December (Day 13) One question answered

A new way to anchor the cruising chute was devised, and this one worked. Although the wind was still not much more than a breeze, we enjoyed good sailing for most of the day, the cruising chute making a real difference and adding at least 2 knots to our boat speed. Suddenly we became aware of another noise, this time from the back of the boat. It was the spool on the fishing rod running freely; Robin had finally caught a fish!

It was a dorado, not huge, but enough for a meal. Friday soon became fry-day as Chris rustled up fish and chips for us all, except for Glyn, who had chips. We kidded ourselves that this was a free meal, given to us by the bounty of the ocean. Later, Robin did a quick back-of-the-envelope calculation. After factoring in the cost of the rod, reel, lines, traces, swivels and lures, all bought for the purpose, he reckoned the cost of our fish and chip supper was about £37 per head. But it did taste great and was worth every penny.

7th December (Day 14) A mixed forecast

Although the wind remained light, the forecast was at last more encouraging, confidently predicting that the long-awaited trade winds would be with us in two or three days' time. Because of the uncertainty, we had done something that we did not think we would do; we had flown the cruising chute right through the previous night. Flying such a sail at night is not normally 'the done thing' as it severely restricts manoeuvrability, but our bit of the ocean had seemed empty and we wanted to make the most of the breeze for as long as it stayed with us.

Even though we were now two full weeks into the rally, we were still not yet headed directly west towards Saint Lucia, but south-west, trying to get closer to where the trade winds would be, once they started to blow. However, we were still closing the gap significantly between where we were and Saint Lucia, but not as directly as the proverbial crow flies.

8th December (Day 15) Half-way there

The lack of wind brought with it one advantage; the sea was as still as a millpond for the first (and last) time in our journey. It was advantageous because we had promised ourselves an ocean swim when we reached the rally half-way point, provided the sea state was suitable, and it was. The water was warm and refreshing. Glyn amazed us, telling us that this was his first dip in any sea since he was about 15 years old! We further celebrated reaching the half-way milestone with Christmas cake and a bottle of red wine and, most refreshing of all, we allowed ourselves half-a-bowl of fresh hot water each for a wash and shave! Nature added to our celebrations by giving us a most glorious sunset, a feast for our eyes.

9th December (Day 16) Flying along against all odds

At 08.00 a surprise wind arrived from an unexpected direction, allowing us some close-hauled sailing. We knew it was a freak wind and, as such, we expected it to stop as quickly as it started; but it did not, and gave us a full 22 hours of great sailing, averaging just over 6 knots of speed.

We should have also landed our second fish. Another dorado, probably four or five-times the size of the one we caught before, had taken the lure and had then given Robin a spirited fight for its freedom. Robin wrestled the thing for some 40 minutes, edging it ever closer to our landing net. But just when we thought we had it, the net failed us and the whopper went its way. I shall not say who was handling the landing net at the time as it would be personally embarrassing, but that fish would have kept Glyn in just chips for the rest of the voyage.

10th December (Day 17) Cruising chute made redundant

Although we did not know it at the time, we would soon be snuffing the cruising chute and bagging it for the last time. It would not be used again for the remainder of the rally. That was the best of times because it meant that the light winds were over and 'proper' winds had taken their place, requiring more robust sails to be deployed. The wind direction was still a bit confused but no-one cared about that. The stronger sails were filled and our speed rarely dipped below 6 knots all day and throughout the night.

During the day, we heard via the VHF radio that, about 200 miles behind us, an abandoned yacht was floating free, its crew of two having been taken aboard a ship for some unknown reason. It was not an ARC yacht. We chatted over the marine salvage rules, which probably run to hundreds of pages but the essence of which are 'finders keepers, losers weepers'. We totted up the advantage, if any, of giving up the rally and going back to see if we could find it, tow it and sell it, but knew in practice that needles in haystacks would be easier to locate. But those were just fleeting thoughts, interrupted by the sound of Robin's fishing spool spinning rapidly again; our second dorado dinner was about to be landed. Three of us ate it with chorizo rice and one of us did not.

11th December (Day 18) Only 1,000 miles to go!

What was happening? The wind, so elusive for so long, was strengthening by the hour, stirring the sea such that it became increasingly rough and lumpy. Even with reefed sails we were still flying along at about 7 knots.

Incidentally, if you have never sailed the seas, 7 knots will sound incredibly slow to you. How could anyone get excited about a speed of little more than 8 miles per hour? But those who sail will know that, with the wind and spray coming at you, 8 miles per hour on an open yacht feels like driving your car in the rain at 88 miles per hour with your head out of the window. And whereas your car can be steered easily, the wind and waves conspire to twist and turn a boat in every direction except the one in which you want it to go, giving the helm a heaviness that has to be fought to stay on course. It may just be 7 knots but, if you enjoy such sailing conditions, it feels more like seventh heaven.

With the ocean offering us no landmarks to steer towards, it was easier to focus on a cloud by day or a star by night rather than keeping a constant eye on the compass. However, I am quite sure that Glyn and Robin were a bit bemused when Chris or I might say to one another something like, "Aim for the rabbit holding a spade." We knew what each other meant because we enjoy pareidolia. Many people share in this but few know it by name; it describes those who, for example, when staring at the clouds or patterned carpets and curtains, see faces, shapes or animals in the patterns. Pareidolia was particularly helpful at sea. Because one cloud looks very much like another one, it was easier to aim at a particular cloud if it happened to look like a pixie or an elephant wearing a hat.

During the night, it was not so easy to make out imaginary images. Instead, we relied more on the moon, stars and planets to give us a helping hand. By fortunate coincidence, the moon happened to set broadly in our direction of travel, providing us with a brightly lit roadway to follow as it made its way down in front of us, clouds permitting. Stars and planets too had their own distinctive patterns, which all helped our navigation. The planet Venus stood out above all the others. Its natural brightness is second only to the moon, so bright in fact that it can cast a shadow. We followed it often. It shone so big and bright that I half-expected it to lead us to Bethlehem, Christmas being just around the corner!

By late evening we had hit the milestone of having only

another 1,000 nautical miles to go. The daft rewards that we had promised ourselves before we had set sail included not playing any reggae music until we had reached this point of the rally. Late as it was, we soon had Bob Marley booming 'No Woman, No Cry' through the speakers. Champagne and mince pies completed our celebrations. It was also time to put the clocks back another hour. I changed my watch but forgot to alter my alarm clock, which led me to get Chris up at 01.00 rather than 02.00, an hour early for his night watch duty. He laughed...eventually.

12ᵗʰ December (Day 19) Easterly winds at last!

The confused winds gave way to a strong easterly; it was without doubt the trade wind for which we had waited so long. And what a wind it was! Blowing 20 knots and gusting much more, it was accompanied by big sea swells. We ran on just the genoa sail, and that well-reefed, yet still maintained a speed of about 7 knots. At last, we had the conditions that we had long expected.

Friday 13ᵗʰ (Day 20) A head full

We had just endured the stormiest of nights, high winds and high seas combined. If you can imagine what it might be like to spend ten hours in a washing machine, that is how it felt to us. We would later learn via the daily ARC radio net that a number of yachts had suffered damage, some serious. One broke its mast, one had its generator washed overboard, one was taking on water and one suffered a fire. Many others had ripped or holed their sails. We were fortunate to have come through unscathed.

That is not to say that we did not have a problem, but it was nothing to do with the storm. We discovered that our loo was well and truly blocked. A lingering smell in the cockpit gave us the first indication, and Chris later confirmed it. Unfortunately, the unblocking process had to be done under the hull, and it was definitely not the weather to go snorkelling. We resigned ourselves to the fact that we would not be able to clear the blockage at sea.

Our only option was to close-off the loo and reinstate the other one that we were using as the food store. We could see Glyn turning physically pale as we dismantled his domain. Every tin, packet, bottle and jar that he had painstakingly counted, categorised and catalogued was now being haphazardly flung to the four corners of the boat wherever space could be found. For some of us, it was urgent; we needed that loo!

While all this activity was happening inside, there was rare activity happening outside too. A large cargo ship had come into view and so had another ARC yacht. Strange as it may seem, we had not seen a single vessel of any sort for the last eight days and nights. Suddenly, like London buses, two had appeared at once. The yacht was called Koala and we would stay in touch by sight or by radio for the remainder of the rally.

14th December (Day 21) Another question answered

"Put a little bit on my plate", said Glyn. Amazingly, he was talking about a tuna that Robin had caught; his third fishing triumph. And Glyn got it down and kept it down! That apart, nothing had changed. The wind was still blowing hard and gusting at gale force, and the sea state was challenging, with big swells restricting our speed, and waves hitting us from every side. The Alton Towers experience continued unabated.

15th December (Day 22) Second Wind damaged

Our original aim had been to cover 120 nautical miles every 24 hours, but that was dashed in those early days of little wind. But we had now covered distances of between 140 and 160 nautical miles for 6 consecutive 24 hour periods; another 3 or so days at that rate of knots would see us home. Although encouraged by the mathematics, we still had our hands full in dealing with the weather. The wind was now blowing 25 knots and more, and our boat was being tossed around such that it was impossible to hold a course without wrestling the wheel continuously.

Something had to give with such violent movements and it turned out to be two of the metal connectors that held the solar-panel frame together. Unbeknown to us, they must have been shaking themselves loose for some time but suddenly both joints came apart, threatening the collapse of the entire gantry. We needed to quickly lash the rest of the frame together; a rope was applied like a tourniquet and twisted tight with the first suitable thing that came to hand; a wooden spoon! It worked so well that we did not bother to try to replace it with anything more suitable, and so the spoon was to stay where it was for the remainder of the rally. That was not the only damage sustained; later we lost the use of our generator when its starting cord broke. It was not at all comfortable (or safe) to work on the generator, sited as it was at the boat's bow, which was pitching wildly as we battled the weather. We therefore decided that we could cope without it for the few remaining days at sea.

Meanwhile, below deck, Glyn was valiantly trying to bake bread when a huge wave sent his bottle of olive oil somersaulting through the air and depositing most of its contents over the floor. There followed a lot of mopping up and not a few 'Popeye and Olive Oil' jokes at Glyn's expense, but all in good humour.

16th December (Day 23) The battle of the helm

The rough weather continued and the confused seas took on the appearance of a seething cauldron; it twisted and turned us at will. It was especially exciting when large waves rolled up behind the boat, picked us up, and then surfed us down the face of the wave, literally doubling our boat-speed for a few seconds. We achieved nearly 13 knots on one such surf, faster than Second Wind had ever gone before under my brother's ownership.

Another new experience for all of us was the great holes in the sea that opened up, seemingly from nowhere. They suddenly appeared, sometimes behind us, sometimes in front, but it was the ones that opened up to the side of us that were the most unnerving. We knew, gravity being what it is, that there was nothing we could do to prevent Second Wind from slipping sideways into those wide watery craters before we were able to regain control again. This happened time and again.

However, it was not all fun. Later in the day, we came as close as we would ever come to a knockdown. Wind gusts were now hitting 40 knots and we knew we needed to reef the sails even further. Just as we started winching, a freak wave struck the rear starboard side of the yacht, skewing her sideways. The full area of our reefed sails was now exposed to the strong wind and that combination of too much wind on too much canvas heeled the boat over at an alarming angle, her portside gunnel well beneath the sea surface.

Frantically we continued to try to reduce sail and steer the boat. We had no doubt that Second Wind's heavy keel would quickly do its work and bring us upright again in a matter of seconds, but we had to ensure that the same wind on the same sail would not simply heel us over again. We came up and carried on. The whole incident had lasted only a matter of seconds, but it had felt much longer. We were learning that ocean sailing in such conditions was relentlessly testing. There was no opportunity to pull in until the storm had passed or to get a good night's sleep and see what the next day might bring. We had to keep battling, day and night, without respite. It was exhilarating but bone-achingly tiring at times.

17th and 18th December (Day 24 and 25) The end is nigh!

The early hours of the morning saw torrential rain come our way, highlighting the one design fault of the Moody 425. Water that falls onto the cockpit bench seats either side of the helm drains away through two small pipes that exit a few inches up from the cockpit floor, immediately above the helmsman's feet. It was no fun in the rain having our deck shoes constantly filled with water from those drain holes. But that was just a small annoyance. It was completely outweighed by knowing that, within a few hours, Saint Lucia would come into view and, in the morning, we should be there. Seeing land again would be salve to our salty eyes.

Christopher Columbus again came to mind. On his first foray across the Atlantic Ocean back in 1492, he had not seen land for five full weeks, nor was he too sure when he would see it. He did not have satellite technology to guide him, relying instead on only his eyes, and those of his crew. Their lucky break was spotting a large flock of birds; Columbus changed course to follow them. They must have known then that land was near. I imagined that everyone who could have been spared, would have been scanning the horizon, their eyes out like organ stops, not least because of the reward that Columbus had offered to the man who saw land first.

Suddenly, a Spanish sailor by the name of Rodrigo de Triana excitedly shouted, "Tierra! Tierra!", his eyes finally fixed on land but his mind more likely fixed on how he might spend that reward of 10,000 marivedis. Whether 10,000 marivedis was a lot or not does not matter to me. Unfortunately for Rodrigo, it did not matter to him either. Crafty Christopher was to later write in his journal that he had actually seen the land a few hours before poor Roddy, but had just not told anyone. He therefore claimed the reward for himself. Nice chap, that Christopher!

Enough of him; now it was our turn, and a good time to run the flag of Saint Lucia up our mast. In yachting, it is a recognised courtesy to fly the flag of the countries you visit. Chris had bought and brought the right flag; our problem was suddenly realising that we did not know which way up it should fly. Too embarrassed to radio ahead and ask a dumb question, we guessed, and raised the flag what we hoped was the right way up. Happily, we would later discover that we had guessed right.

As we sailed ever nearer to our destination, we were faced with the same slightly-annoying time issue as when we had approached the Cape Verde Islands. We were again in danger of arriving too early in the pitch dark before dawn on the Wednesday. Once again, we deliberately slowed our pace a little. As the night passed, we saw the distinctive shape of Pigeon Island emerge from the morning mist. That was not the first sight of soil that came into view but it was the bit of land that we were aiming for, on Saint Lucia's northernmost tip.

The name Pigeon Island is today something of a misnomer in that the message-carrying pigeons after which it was named are no longer launched from its high points, and also, although it was an island for thousands of years, a causeway was constructed in the early 1970s, joining it to the Saint Lucia mainland. So Pigeon Island is now a pigeon-less non-island. Its importance to us was that Rodney Bay, our ultimate destination, was just the other side of it.

Its twin peaks are what gives Pigeon Island its distinctive shape. The higher is known as Signal Hill and it was from here, back in the 1770s, that Admiral George Rodney could keep an eye on the French naval base on the island of Martinique, which was just in view on a clear day. Back then, the French were enemies of England whereas now, they just do not like us very much. It was because Admiral Rodney orchestrated a spectacular defeat of the French navy that the bay to the west of Pigeon Island still carries his name today.

The ARC finishing line was around the other side of the

headland but sailing that last section of the rally required a final rig change, taking down our spinnaker pole and sailing the final mile or so close-hauled as we turned towards the wind.

For some time we had been able to hear the finishing line team calling up a number of yachts over the radio. They, of course, knew what we did not know, and that was where every yacht was in relation to us. It transpired that more than a dozen yachts were all within a few miles of each other, converging on the finishing line over those early morning hours.

One of them was Koala, the yacht we had played cat and mouse with over the past half-dozen days, Second Wind generally moving ahead during the daytimes and Koala overtaking us during the nights. As the night was only just passing, Koala had once again moved ahead of us, although it appeared to us that her windvane steering system had seemingly taken her too far north, towards Martinique. However, as we all but stopped to change our rig, we saw that Koala's apparent deviation was tactical, enabling her to use the prevailing wind and tide to make a final surge towards the finish, leaving us in her wake. And we thought they were our friends! Would we have done the same to them, given half a chance? Of course!

At the crew's insistence, Chris took over the helm as we neared the finishing line. It was his boat, his idea to sail the Atlantic and by his invitation that the rest of us were there at all; his should be the honour of helming Second Wind to victory. For us, of course, victory meant not arriving in last place or after the celebratory bunting had been taken down. We were about to achieve that victory on both counts.

Chapter Six

No pressure, no problem

Wonderful words

"Second Wind. Congratulations. You have now crossed the finishing line. Welcome to Saint Lucia. Welcome to America. Now enjoy your life."

Those were the words that we heard over our radio as Second Wind crossed the finishing line. We did not know the man behind the voice, and could only guess as to how he might look, but his words were music to our ears. We had completed our challenge.

The first person to congratulate us face-to-face was the official photographer. He was clearly adept at photographing boats at sea from his one-man rubber dinghy in which he came out to meet us, standing up, steering via an extended tiller in one hand, the other hand working his large, shoulder-mounted camera. Although he came to photograph our finish, we found ourselves taking pictures of him, impressed by his balance and boat-skills.

After he had taken all the action shots he needed, we furled our sails and motored the short distance towards the Rodney Bay marina. Being early morning, the local fishermen were going in the opposite direction, on their way out to sea in their colourful open boats, no doubt to catch dorados of their own. They too appeared genuinely enthusiastic as they waved to us and shouted their congratulations, one tapping his watch and telling us through a wide grin that we had been expected sooner. Everyone seemed very cheerful considering the earliness of the hour.

A different voice then spoke over the radio waves, telling us that a berthing place had been allocated to Second Wind alongside one of the long quays normally reserved for super-yachts twice her length. It seemed we were going to have posh neighbours. As we approached, another ARC yacht that had finished just ahead of us – Spirit of Islay – was already moored at one end of the quay, leaving us just enough space to fit Second Wind on the outer end. Robin took over the helm and reversed us expertly to where we needed to be.

Waiting to take our lines and offer his own congratulations was one of the ARC's yellow-shirted team members, there to meet and greet us. It was reassuring to see those yellow shirts again. Within minutes, Second Wind was moored and we stepped onto solid ground for the first time in many a day. And the ground really was solid; the quay was made of concrete. My head was telling me that it was simply impossible for concrete to move a single inch, yet it definitely seemed to be swaying quite a lot! It was not just me; we all felt the sway, and staggered a little as we found our balance. The apparent swaying is known as land-sickness and is much easier to bear than its sea-sickness cousin.

Just then, another jovial local greeted us. From the small trolley he was pushing, he presented us with a basket of fresh fruit and a bottle of something alcoholic. He then handed each of us a cup of ice-cold rum punch, the traditional ARC welcome.

It is a well-known fact that sailors down through the ages have enjoyed a long association with rum, but even they had to wait until 'the sun was over the yardarm' before drinking it. Yardarms were the horizontal spars mounted on the masts of old sailing ships from which the sails were hung. It could be argued, of course, that the sun could appear over the topmost yardarm at almost any time of day, depending where you were in the world, but it is generally accepted that the expression originated in the North Atlantic, indicating that no alcoholic drink would be taken before something like 11 o'clock in the morning.

Well for us, it was nothing like 11 o'clock; indeed the sun was barely up, let alone above anything, but it was a lovely way to be welcomed and we drank the punch in the spirit in which it was given. Although beyond my personal experience, I understood that alcohol could also make things appear to sway so, as things were already swaying, perhaps it would make them stop. It did not. I later learned that the Royal Navy did away with rum rations back in 1970, apparently worried about its effect on sailors using machinery. I would have thought that its effect on sailors firing guns should have been more of a concern, but what do I know?

As soon as our welcome party had dispersed, our priority was to call up our loved ones on the phone. We knew that those back home would be aware already that we had arrived through following our progress on the online Fleet Tracker facility, but it was still a joy to confirm our arrival and, better still, to promise to be home for Christmas after all.

Next on our agenda was a trip to the shower facilities. I appreciate I have been a little disparaging about the quality of marina showers in previous pages, but no such comments will now pass my lips. Frankly, if it had just been a rusty pipe sticking out of the ground it would not have mattered. Just standing under a stream of fresh, hot water was heaven on earth.

Similarly for the loo. Earlier I made the mistake of saying that my first lavatory experience in a Las Palmas marina would make using the heads on a yacht a doddle, even in the stormiest of seas. I said that because, at the time, I had never been in the stormiest of seas. And I still have not, but the storms we did endure were enough to convince me that I was wrong. During our volatile voyage, Robin even coined a new phrase for using the heads, saying on his way that he was going "to go ten rounds with the kick boxer." That was how it felt. While confined to that tiny space in heavy weather, we had been slammed against walls, injured by the towel holder, impaled on the door handle, stabbed by the coat hooks and generally thrown about every which way, emerging battered and bruised. Such was our concentration on protecting ourselves in that little cubicle that I was sure we sometimes forgot why we were there in the first place. But now, any movement was simply imaginary and we could sit serenely still, knowing the only danger was falling asleep and causing a queue.

The carnival continues

The carnival atmosphere that the World Cruising Club had so effectively created in Las Palmas was just as effectively re-created in Saint Lucia. Dress flags once again fluttered from the many ARC yachts already moored. Either side of the marina's main walkway, colourful huts had been erected displaying local produce, paintings, arts and crafts and other local novelty items. Interspersed were tents and cabins selling a variety of food and drinks. In the middle of this ARC village was a bandstand from which live music was frequently performed, including the wonderful sound of Caribbean steel drums.

Behind the many temporary structures were the marina's permanent shops and cafés, festooned with Christmas decorations and tempting us with, among many other things, full English breakfasts! Oscar Wilde once said that he could resist everything except temptation, and we proved him right when it came to those breakfast offers.

But all of that would have been nothing without the people. Those who live and work on the island were both welcoming and friendly, rarely without a smile. Their watchwords appeared to be, "No pressure, no problem", a phrase we heard repeatedly. Even the handlebars on their bicycles were swept well back enabling the riders to be just as laid-back when cycling as they were by nature. Their hospitality was much appreciated.

The other people who made our stay so memorable were of course the ARC crews. They were everywhere, and the happy chatter of the pre-rally events resumed, but with one noticeable difference; gone was any trace of apprehension. That was all behind us. Everyone there was there because they had made it, and we all had our stories to tell and fish sizes to exaggerate.

In addition, there was the post-rally programme of ARC-organised activities to enjoy. Our later-than-expected arrival meant we missed out on some of the early events, including that Hog Roast we had initially aimed for, but there was yet another fancy dress party, this one held on a beach at Pigeon Island. As well as live music, we were entertained by acrobats and fire-eaters. Then one of the singers moved among the crowd, inviting anyone who knew the words to the song to take over the mic. There was no holding him back; in an instant, Robin had grabbed the mic and was belting out another Marley favourite, Everything's Gonna Be Alright. And it was.

Prizes galore

The climax of the ARC events was the awards ceremony hosted by Andrew Bishop, Managing Director of the World Cruising Club. This was held on the 21st December after the finishing line had officially closed and with only a handful of yachts still on their way. Hundreds of people crammed the venue and applauded enthusiastically as more than 200 prizes were awarded. The prizes recognised not just the winners and runners up in each of the boat categories, but also the many people who had helped by, for example, manning the finishing line or organising the various daily ARC radio nets, or the people who took the best photo, caught the biggest fish, wrote the best log, and so on.

Memorably, the best video prize went to a brave crew-member who held his waterproof camera under the water to film a hammerhead shark swimming just a few meters behind his boat and looking every bit as frightening as you would imagine. The biggest fish caught was a white marlin weighing in at 45 kilos, certainly far beyond anything our flimsy landing net could have handled. And the most original log was one written by the skipper of the catamaran Ula. Under the pseudonym of D Salinator, he wrote it from the perspective of being a watermaker. It may help to know that watermakers are hugely expensive and yet notorious for breaking down. Ula's amusing log is reproduced in full at the end of this book, together with three of our own.

We learned that the youngest person to cross the ocean in the rally was just two years old. Perhaps more astounding was that the youngest skipper was just 19! Chris was no doubt encouraged to learn that the oldest skipper was a full 16 years his senior and that 77 of the skippers were 60 or over, although that will not stop me from making fun of his age. Andrew Bishop also mentioned that the Fleet Tracker web page had received over 272,000 'hits' during the rally; we may have felt alone on the ocean waves, but there were clearly many folk back home following our progress.

The one thing we were told that we knew already was that the 2013 ARC Rally had been one of the most challenging rallies of recent years, with the majority of yachts taking longer than usual to make the crossing due to, first, the lack of wind, and then the powerful strength of the wind. Incredibly, however, the racers did set a new record of 10 days, 21 hours, 25 minutes and 10 seconds! None of the cruisers came close to that time yet, to our surprise, the Cruising Division winner only just pipped Second Wind by a mere 124 places!

The loud cheers and spontaneous applause throughout the ceremony event made it a fitting end to a wonderful adventure and a well-deserved tribute to the energy and hard work of the ARC team for organising it for us. And as if to give us a final reminder of some of the sailing conditions we had experienced, torrential rain suddenly interrupted the half-time interval just as we were all outside enjoying food and live entertainment. The rain sent everyone scurrying for shelter but did nothing to diminish the fun of the whole evening and the memories we would all take home with us.

Out and About

Our short stay in Saint Lucia was rounded off with two days of sight-seeing. Once famous for sugar production, the beautiful island is now a land of bananas and mangoes, rum and reggae. If I was speaking to that South African skipper who had bemoaned Britain's empire building of the past, I could have honestly told him that Great Britain never once conquered the island, but that would have been a tad misleading. It was true to say 'never once' because GB actually conquered it seven times between the late 1600s and early 1800s, the French wresting back control in between. It would be churlish to say which country eventually won that territorial tug of war, but it is the face of our Queen on the island's currency today. Whatever its history, Saint Lucia is a lovely land, and we were glad of the chance to see at least some of it.

Jane, this time with daughter Sophie, and Angela had once again flown out to where we were, and they had organised a fantastic sight-seeing itinerary for us all. First we visited a secluded beach, sat in the shade of its palm trees and swam in the warm waters of its bay. Sea swimming for Glyn was in danger of becoming a habit, with two dips in quick succession, following his prior interlude of some 40 years.

The seven of us then enjoyed a catamaran trip that took us two-thirds of the way down the west coast of Saint Lucia. It made a nice change for someone else to be hauling up the sails for us, although Glyn did persuade the captain to let him take over the helm for most of the way. The catamaran brought us to the ancient town of Soufrière, which had been the island's capital city when in French hands. Following the French Revolution of 1789, it was to Soufrière that the gruesome guillotine was brought and set up in the town square to see an end to many a Royalist. Today the enemies of Soufrière are natural ones; the hurricanes that routinely cause significant damage every few years, and the occasional forest fire or mud slide.

The town stands in the shadow of Saint Lucia's famous Piton mountains that are depicted by two of the triangles on the island's flag; had we known that, of course, we would have known which way up to fly it. Our tour continued by minibus, and we enjoyed a swim beneath a waterfall, a dip in the sulphur pools and a guided tour of an old plantation, learning how coconuts were peeled and how chocolate was made in bygone days. Better still, we were invited to taste the fresh coconut and the chocolate-flavoured cocoa beans. Back in the bay, Glyn took yet another dip in the sea as we all enjoyed a time of snorkelling before the catamaran sailed us home, its captain leading everyone in some riotous dancing on the way. Those Saint Lucians certainly know how to have fun!

The following day we discovered Angela and Jane's itinerary had left the best till last. We found ourselves being driven up through Saint Lucia's rain forest to an array of zip wires strung across the top of the tree canopy. For the next couple of hours, it was our great pleasure to zip ourselves over the spectacular scenery of high tress, deep valleys and running water. I say, 'zip ourselves', but in reality, Jane zipped herself down only one of the twelve wires. That was no small achievement in itself, but she somehow managed to orchestrate things such that she zipped the other eleven wires in the arms of a rather handsome young instructor! While the rest of us steered and braked for ourselves, Jane just had to lay back and enjoy the rides. No wonder she was smiling. No pressure, no problem!

Final reflections

It would be wrong to leave the impression that everything about our adventure was easy; some aspects were not. But challenges would not be challenges without difficulties. Those 'no wind' days were not easy; we learned that a depression in the weather leads to a depression in the crew too. We had planned so well for the physical challenge but I dare say we should have been better prepared for the emotional one. That said, only minor niggles ever surfaced. In Saint Lucia we did hear stories of World War Three breaking out on a couple of yachts, but happily that was the exception rather than the rule.

Going without enough sleep was also not easy. That, of course, is well known, which is why sleep deprivation is recognised as an instrument of torture. The difference is, unscrupulous regimes do it to others; we did it to ourselves! Our 'four hours on, four hours off' watch pattern works well for a voyage of a few days, but we had to maintain it for not far short of a month, and it began to take its toll on the heaviness of our eyelids. Talking of heaviness, perhaps it is a good time to sneak in the answer to the weight gain or weight loss question: Despite our eyelids getting heavier, my overall weight dropped by about three-quarters of a stone over the course of the crossing. I suspected as much early on when my shorts started to slip down my legs, and it was confirmed by my bathroom scales as soon as I arrived home.

Speaking of home, missing it is the final example I will give of things that were not easy. It was not just that we missed those we love or family events, tough though that was; it was much more than that. The ocean became our whole world and as such we were detached from everything else. Sure, things continued to happen in the world at large, but because we did not get to hear of them, we could not react to them in the normal way. The home-call of that great statesman, Nelson Mandela is a good example. His death occurred while we were at sea. Not being around to hear the tributes, to see the newscasts, to read the articles, to remind ourselves of his most remarkable life or to feel his loss left us somehow diminished.

Having said all of that, not one of us has the slightest regret about taking part in the rally. Any sadness, sickness, strain or struggle that we might have felt pales against the many highlights that will remain with us. We have seen sunrises and sunsets of breathtaking beauty, and scenery which was simply stunning; we have seen night-skies with more clarity and depth of wonder than the land's light-pollution ever allows; we have seen the awesome skills of birds and dolphins, gracing the sky and sea. We have seen places that we never expected to visit and met people from cultures so different to our own.

And although it was not the plan, the confused winds that came at us from every direction meant that we experienced every point of sail during our time at sea, rather than just sailing with the wind behind us the whole way, as had been expected. I confess that when I started, being the novice, I could not quite properly comprehend how a yacht could, by and large, keep the same course irrespective of the direction of the wind. But now I understand. As Ella Wheeler Wilcox put it in 1916:

One ship sails East,
And another West,
By the self-same winds that blow,
'Tis the set of the sails
And not the gales,
That tells the way we go.

I remain the novice as I would still need to mug-up quite a bit to gain any qualifications, but with well over 4,000 nautical miles of ocean sailing under my belt, I do now understand how to set the sails, and the thrill of getting it right and feeling the boat respond will remain with me.

What a pleasure and privilege it has been for the crew of Second Wind, together planning and carrying through a challenge that so few in the world will ever do. We have battled against winds and waves beyond our previous experiences, and come through smiling. We have learned new things about ocean sailing and about ourselves. We have tested ourselves, each in his own way, and passed. We have met great people, enjoyed great parties, had great conversations and now have great memories and stories to tell. And throughout, we have leaned heavily on the ARC team's know-how, support and organisational talents; they above all have come through with flying colours.

The bond that develops within the ARC family is best illustrated by the arrival in Saint Lucia of the yacht, Beagle. You will not find Beagle's name in the pecking order of the 2013 ARC results because she did the two things that we did not want to do. One, she came in last, on Christmas Day in fact, days after the formal finishing line had closed. Two, not only had the bunting been taken down but the entire ARC village had been dismantled by then. Understandably, the husband and wife crew thought they would slip into Rodney Bay unannounced and unnoticed. Not a bit of it. Almost 100 ARC crew who were spending Christmas in Saint Lucia made their way to the pontoons, some with flags, others with their compressed-air fog horns, and they gave Beagle a welcome fit for a winner. That again was the spirit of the ARC shining through.

One last question: Would we do it again?

We asked one another this very question, and the answers differ. Chris had only ever intended to do it just the once, so his response is 'probably not' although he really enjoyed the whole experience and loves the long days away from anything and everything. When pushed, he did concede that if, say, his son or daughter was keen to do it, he could easily let himself be talked into repeating the ARC at some time in the future.

When Robin was asked, he did not quite respond with Sir Steve Redgrave's famous words after winning gold at the 1996 Atlanta Olympics, "If anyone sees me go anywhere near a boat, you've got my permission to shoot me", but his answer was still a 'No'. On the face of it, this may be surprising given that, out of Robin, Glyn and me, Robin is the most likely to buy a boat of his own. Nothing he has experienced with the ARC, including his sea-sickness, has put him off his love of sailing, but ocean sailing is not what he enjoys the most. His preference is to have a yacht somewhere nearer to home, race it when the opportunity arises, but mostly sail it during the day and moor it somewhere for the night, enjoying a meal onshore and a good night's sleep before sailing off again the next day.

Glyn's answer is also 'No' but for different reasons. For him it was a challenge and, in one respect, more of a challenge than for the rest of us, given his diabetes. When we attended the First Aid course back in the spring of 2013, the tutor even expressed some surprised concern that he was doing it at all, knowing the disruption the rally would cause to his sleeping and eating patterns. But as it turned out, Glyn coped quietly and effectively with managing his condition and as such, is an example to those who are tempted to cite their diabetes as their reason for not doing things. With careful planning, it can be done, and Glyn has proved it. Glyn's nature, however, is not to repeat the same challenge but to look for something different, whatever that might be. That said, if no other challenge came his way and he had the chance of sailing the ARC again, I am certain he would.

And me? It was a wonderful experience, a fantastic challenge and I am thrilled to have done it. In one way, I cannot imagine how such an opportunity would ever present itself again so I could give any answer, knowing it will probably never be tested. And being honest, like Robin, given the choice between ocean sailing and day sailing, the latter has a lot going for it. But I am still mindful of those countless thousands I mentioned in the opening paragraph of this book; people who would love to do what we had just done, but will never get the chance. Remembering them, I just know that I would say 'Yes' again, if ever that privilege came my way.

The odd thing is, if we had asked ourselves the same question part way through the rally, we would probably have all said 'No', especially during those tough days. But there is something about the ocean that makes you forget the worst of times and remember the best of times. I cannot explain it. What makes it even more inexplicable is that only certain people feel it. Some folk would never even read a little book like this about sailing, let alone get on a yacht. And it is way beyond their comprehension why anyone would willingly do what we put ourselves through. They like the seaside, even paddle in the shallows, but nothing more; they are certainly not inwardly drawn to the deep blue. But others are so drawn. It is like magnetism. Just being near a boat triggers a longing to head off to new horizons. Where that longing comes from, I do not know. According to the poet, Henry Wadsworth Longfellow, it is a secret.

... my soul is full of longing
For the secret of the sea,
And the heart of the great ocean
Sends a thrilling pulse through me.

All I know is that I too feel that thrilling pulse!

Appendix

The log opposite won the ARC prize for being the most original and simply the best. It was written by Paul McMorris, skipper of the catamaran, Ula, and was posted on the World Cruising Club website on 29th November 2013. It is reproduced here with his kind permission. Paul's clever angle was to write it from the perspective of Ula's aged and temperamental watermaker. Paul sails Ula with his wife, Tanya. We on Second Wind got to know them well during our ARC adventure, and we were glad we did; they were good mates to us, and made a great team together. We thank them, and wish them fair winds and following seas, always.

The Watermaker

I am a watermaker. And I am sad.

Lately I have become a problem to my man-user. I have become a saga, and I fear that this time will soon be referred to as Water'maker' Gate. You see, though I was working fine, and although I had never missed a beat, I had a few ailments. Sure I leaked here and there, and I bounced around a bit on my aching joints. But I am no spring chicken. No, I may not have the automatic-fresh-flush-system, and no, I may not have the remote-start-panel like today's youngsters, but I am simple, and robust, tried and tested, and dependable.

Nonetheless, Skip broke the golden rule. Don't fix it if it ain't bust! He sent a strange man-doctor to visit me. To my surprise he told Skip that I had become lethargic, and wasn't making fresh water, rather that I was passing off some slightly-less-salty-than-sea-water as fresh water! Who does he think he is? This is my only job. I know what I'm doing!

I protested when I was taken to hospital on a man-island. There, Skip was told my situation was worse than feared, and that I may soon visit the watermaker heaven. Thankfully, the chief engineer didn't see it necessary to enlist the services of the expensive younger generation, so I was to be healed. I had experience in my role! These youngsters have seen no service. I have served, and have earned respect! I was to be saved.

So I had bypass surgery, cosmetic surgery and I was feeling

genuinely rejuvenated. Ironically though, it was my man-doctor that then became lethargic, and he decided he wanted nothing more to do with me! So he deposited me, in pieces, beside my ship, and left me there.

Skip and chief engineer didn't leave me though, by the quayside, like some discarded empty Evian bottle. They took me back and reinstated me, despite it being the day before our departure...

Why do man people need to move from one man-island to another? They are strange. Me, I have a good day if I simply make water! It's my purpose, my meaning of being.

Now, man-people do not talk to me much, but when they do, the air is usually blue as they coax me into life. But Skip and chief engineer - I have never heard the like of it! I was lambasted for a whole day as they reassembled all my pieces! The man-doctor was mentioned much of the time. I liked him. He tried to help me get well. I do not think they like him or respect him much.

Finally I was back. I looked good, and I felt great. I wanted to show off my new prowess. Unfortunately, my inauguration released some more foul language from Skip and chief engineer as my feed pump burned out, and my HP sensor failed. And I still leaked... I didn't see any man-people for a while.

Skip and chief engineer still didn't leave me though. I like them. They respect me. They helped me get well again.

So we left on schedule. But I have lost their trust. I heard them talking about diverting to some other man islands, where they would take on some extra water. That's my job! Let me work! I will produce water, and lots of it! Still their confidence in me is broken.

But I am strong again! I know it! I can feel the strength in my ceramic cylinders! My joints no longer ache, and I do not leak! But Skip will not let me loose. He will not push me, rather he pokes and prods, he umms and ahhs and calculates. He thinks I have become a bit hot-headed, and will break if I get my way. I am not hot-headed. The man person - my creator - he told Skip my hot-headedness was normal. But Skip is cautious. The man-doctor hurt him. He doesn't want to be hurt again. He doesn't want to hurt me either. He respects me.

I hear we are no longer diverting to the man islands, perhaps I am beginning to gain trust?

Still, I feel like I have let my crew down. Perhaps soon I can prove myself dependable again.

I am a watermaker, and I am sad.

D Salinator

This log was created by Chris, Second Wind's skipper and owner. During our voyage, he would often start to quote poetry before realising that he did not know the words after all, but muddled through just the same. This log was posted on 3rd December 2013 and follows the style of Lewis Carroll's famous Jabberwocky, albeit very, very loosely. It is reproduced here with massive apologies to all poetry lovers.

Jabberyachty

Twas brillig and the slopping seas
didst slosh and slap upon the ship,
all flimsy was the fitful breeze
and the drooped sails a'dip.

Beware the forecasters my friends
the lines that point, the high and low,
beware the news of trading winds
while feeble vespers blow.

We sailed our spangled barques abroad
long time to reach the windward isle,
while breathless fickle breeze conspires
to torture every mile.

Slip slap slip slap
the struggling sail goes taught and jerks,
while grumbling in the barkys bowels
the iron mainsail works.

And will we make the windward isle?
Of course we will my sailing friends,
a frabscious day twill be we say
when we reach the other end.

This was one of Robin's logs, posted on 11th December 2013. Mindful of those clever yacht names mentioned in Chapter One, Robin's O-Fish-L business on Second Wind was providing Meals-on-Reels, at which he became E-Fishient. He was at first reticent to draft a log but, after Chris encouraged him to Mullet Over, he did, and this was it.

Charged with the responsibility of catching fish for the ship's kitchen and not knowing much about sea fishing, my reading and research led to the purchase of a travel adapted boat rod, multiplier trolling reel, high breaking strain lines with miscellaneous traces, swivels and lures etc. For the first week nothing happened, then suddenly the reel screamed! The boat was doing 7 knots one way and whatever I had hooked was going like a train the other! Result: broken line and broken reel. However our resourceful skipper has a huge collection of spare parts on board and is apparently able to repair almost any mechanical device, so I was soon able to fish on.

Next day, another take on a small lure resulted in a much smaller fish which I was finally successful in reeling in! Simply cooked by baking in lemon and butter it made a fabulous supper for 3 of our crew. Cost per head - £37! Well no one said sailing holidays were cheap. I need to catch more!

Glyn's several logs invariably centred on food, reflecting his role as Second Wind's Provisioning Officer. This one was posted on 9th December 2013. In it, he takes on the persona of an onion; not just any onion, but one with attitude! During the rally, onions easily proved themselves the most durable of all the vegetables, but maybe not the most popular. This is reflected in Glyn's log, in which he demonstrates his uncanny ability to occasionally adopt the mind-set of a vegetable!

I wake from the nightmare. The baleful looks, the accusing eyes. 21 perfect onions look out from the storage nets. "So", they say, "you had the good times with all that fancy fruit and veg but where are they now? Gone! Gone into cakes and crumbles. And now you must confront us. We are still hard enough but are you? Last night you baked a creamy pasta with ham and pea with a breadcrumb and blue cheese crust and a garlic bruschetta. You've been to the River Café too often Jamie. And did you think to use an onion? No, not good enough for your fancy food. Well, not too many veg options left now, eh matey? How are you going to make tinned mince interesting? Might need an onion or two? Well maybe we'll be out that night." The nightmare fades but the onions remain. Don't cry for me...

07766 450805   Rog
01883 373 565

07821 224204

Lightning Source UK Ltd.
Milton Keynes UK
UKOW05f2248160414
230091UK00001B/1/P

9 780755 216390